AF394651

TEN TRANSPORT PIONEERS
WHO CHANGED THE WORLD

TEN TRANSPORT PIONEERS

WHO CHANGED THE WORLD

ANTHONY BURTON

First published 2026

The History Press
97 St George's Place, Cheltenham,
Gloucestershire, GL50 3QB
www.thehistorypress.co.uk

British Library Cataloguing in Publication Data.
A catalogue record for this book is available from the British Library.

ISBN 978 1 80399 947 0

Typesetting and origination by The History Press
Printed and bound in Great Britain by TJ Books, Padstow, Cornwall.

The History Press proudly supports

Trees for Life

www.treesforlife.org.uk

EU Authorised Representative: Easy Access System Europe
Mustamäe tee 50, 10621 Tallinn, Estonia
gpsr.requests@easproject.com

CONTENTS

INTRODUCTION

There have been many inventions and developments that have made major differences in the ways in which we move ourselves and our goods and chattels around. Some, however, happened so long ago that we have no means of knowing exactly how they first came about.

Somewhat surprisingly, the earliest known representation of artificial devices for helping people to move around shows a man on skis. This was carved into a rock face in Norway in the Mesolithic period, which ended in Europe some 8,000 years ago. But if one had to pick just one device that made a fundamental change, it would surely be the wheel. A circular disc, either moving with an axle or moving freely, seems to have first appeared in the Sumer region of Mesopotamia over 5,000 years ago. But how did it evolve? It must have become obvious before that, when huge stones had to be moved for example, that pushing them onto rounded logs and rolling them along, shifting the logs in front as the stone moved, was a good deal more efficient than simply dragging the stone over the ground. But creating efficient wheels and mounting them on axles is a huge step in technology.

Heavy weights can be moved, provided you have enough people to shift them. The alternative is to use stronger animals to do the job for you. Writing in Volume 1 of the *Oxford History of Technology*, S.M. Cole wryly notes that 'man's oldest beast of burden was woman', but there is evidence of asses taking over that role as early as 3000 BCE, and at some stage, someone developed a method of harnessing animals. Artificial tracks, such as the so-called Sweet Path on the Somerset Levels, date back even further, dated to around 3800 BCE.

Roads and vehicles have developed over thousands of years, but evolution was slow. An ancient Egyptian, should he have been brought back to life in the eighteenth century, would not have been astonished by the sight of a horse and cart. Had he arrived just a few decades later, the steam locomotive would have amazed him.

When it comes to floating out on lakes and rivers, the distant past is equally anonymous. How the first primitive boats emerged must have depended on the materials available in any one region. In wooded areas, early humans would have seen logs floating and possibly decided to try to hitch a ride to move downstream and would then have discovered the truth of the saying, 'as easy as falling off a log'. If, however, they lashed the logs together and made a raft, or hollowed one out to create a boat, life afloat would have been easier and a good deal safer. Then, at some stage, it would have become obvious that life could be made even easier if some sort of sail was used. In ancient Egypt, boats were made from reeds and a carving on a tomb at Deir el-Gebrawi of *c.*2400 BCE shows a reed boat with a tripod mast, a yardarm at the top and a triangular sail. This is quite sophisticated, so there must have been earlier, cruder versions.

Over the centuries, transport on land and sea saw many improvements, but we sadly never know anything about the individuals who made crucial breakthroughs. Instead, we have what appears to be a period of steady evolution, rather than revolution. As a result, the accounts that follow cover only a fraction of that long period. We must wait until the time when we begin written records, and even then, more centuries were to pass before anyone thought it necessary to put a name to an invention. We must move forward around 4,500 years from that first-known wheel to start our story of inventors and innovators, and the story will start in the world of sailing ships.

In the following pages, as well as looking at the lives of the pioneers, I shall be putting them in the context of the situation as it existed in their field when they began to think about innovations, and show how their work led on to future developments.

1

JOHN HARRISON

*The inventor of the marine chronometer,
which enabled seamen to calculate their longitude.*

Before turning to our main subject, it helps to know how
things had developed in the world of ships and seamanship
in the many centuries that had passed since the first vessels set
out on the open seas. The development of the sailing ship is a
story of slow evolution rather than revolution, developing in
different ways in different regions.

When Henry VIII ordered ships for what would eventually become the Royal Navy, they carried a complex system
of sails. For his flagship, *Henry Grace à Dieu*, the shipwrights
brought in elements from the northern tradition of square sails
and the Middle-Eastern triangular or lateen sails. The vessel
had a mixture of the two types carried on four masts, with
square sails on the two forward and lateen on the aft.

The master shipwright at the time was James Baker, but
it was his son, Matthew, born around 1530, who made the
first real difference to the way in which ships were designed.
He was to follow his father in the role of Royal Shipwright,

serving under Elizabeth I. Before that, designing a ship was a matter of rule of thumb and an accepted system of correct proportions. The shipwright would set out the central ribs of the ship and wooden templates were set at regular intervals, forward to the bows and back to the stern. Baker's innovation was to devise a system for setting out the ship's lines on paper. These would be drawn as segments of a circle using massive compasses, which would then be used to make templates. The huge advantage of this system was that the designer could make changes easily on paper and produce accurate outlines for every single rib, simply by numbering them on the drawing.

We know quite a lot about Baker's methods, thanks to Samuel Pepys, who is best known as a diarist, but who had been appointed Clerk to the Navy Board in 1658 and collected together Baker's writings, which he named *Fragments*

Tudor shipwrights laying out the lines for a ship from Matthew Baker's *Fragments of Ancient Shipwrighting* of 1586. (The Masters and Fellows, Magdalene College, Cambridge)

of Ancient Shipwrighting. Among the papers were drawings, including an enigmatic one showing a fish superimposed on a ship's hull, perhaps intended to indicate that for smooth movement through the water the hull should be as smoothly streamlined as the fish. There are also many examples of how he believed arithmetic and geography should be used in ship design, including some complex equations and solving cube roots, probably a task beyond most working shipwrights at the time.

Baker's other contribution was to come up with a method of describing the size of a vessel, which he called its 'tunnage' – not a measurement of weight, but of how many tuns (barrels) of wine could be fitted in it. It was, of course, the forerunner of the modern term, 'tonnage', now based on the metric ton.

These were important changes, but even as late as 1819, when Rees's *Cyclopaedia* appeared, the article on naval architecture suggested that although mathematical ideas had been introduced, 'their discoveries are so much enveloped in profound calculations, that shipbuilders, in general, have scarcely been able to derive any advantage from them'. It seems the old ways continued to be used well after Baker's time. Nevertheless, thanks to Baker, the best shipwrights had a far more sophisticated way of designing a vessel than had been possible before.

There was one aspect of seamanship where change was essential. In the early years, when ships set out for foreign lands, they relied very much on landmarks to know exactly where they were. By the eighteenth century, ship's officers had several aids to navigation. They had a compass to tell them in which direction the ship was pointing and they could discover their speed by means of a log. This may have originally been just that, but it was later more sophisticated and was simply a shaped float attached to a line, with knots tied at measured distances apart. The log was thrown overboard and as the ship moved away, the line was let out and the number of knots that passed in a given time provided the speed in nautical miles per hour – knots – a speed that would be entered in the logbook.

There was one other vital piece of information available. A device could be used to measure the angle of the sun above the horizon at noon. There was no need for a clock to tell them when it was noon – it was simply when the sun was at its highest. This measurement gave the latitude.

It might be that knowing where the ship was pointing, how fast it was going and its latitude would be quite enough for anyone to know their position on the sea. But there is a problem. The direction in which the bow is pointing is not necessarily the way the ship is heading. Wind and waves may be pushing it sideways, so that it might be moving several degrees off its compass heading, and over a period of time that could bring the vessel miles off its intended course. The result could be disastrous, as was tragically demonstrated on 22 October 1707.

A British squadron of twenty-one ships was returning from the Siege of Toulon. They were headed by *Association*, under Captain Edmund Loades, with Admiral of the Fleet Sir Cloudesley Shovell on board. They believed themselves to be well out to sea, heading safely for port on the English coast, but were in fact heading towards the Scilly Isles. *Association* hit the Gilstone Rocks, a reef to the west of St Agnes. The St Agnes Light was spotted and warning cannon shots were fired, but too late to save *Association*, which hit the rocks and sank immediately. Three other ships, *Eagle*, *Rodney* and *Firebrand*, also sank. The total number of lives lost has never been accurately measured but estimates vary between 1,300 and 2,000. According to legend, Sir Cloudesley Shovell made it safely to land, but was spotted by a local woman, who murdered him and took his valuable jewelled ring. However, it seems highly unlikely that a man wearing a full admiral's uniform could swim more than a mile to shore.

How did the disaster happen? There are many theories, but no answers. Some have suggested faulty compasses might have been involved, poor charts were being used, an unusually strong current swept them off course and so on. Others have suggested negligence by the ship's officers. Whatever the reason, one thing we do know is that had they had an accurate measure of their longitude, the disaster would never have happened. But that was one thing, at that time, that no naval officer could work out with any degree of accuracy.

There was no immediate response to the accident, but there was a growing feeling among seafarers that their safety depended on being able to solve this problem. A petition was sent to Parliament and, in 1714, a Parliamentary Committee was set up to examine the question; leading scientists of the day were consulted, including the greatest of them all, Sir Isaac Newton. He was well aware that there was a direct relationship between longitude and time. The earth rotates at a regular speed, which means that noon at one longitude will be different from that at another and a one-hour difference corresponds to 15 degrees of longitude. If an accurate timepiece is carried on a ship and set to the time at the home port with a known longitude, then the time difference gives the new longitude. It is not quite that simple – but that is the general principle. He pointed this out to the committee, but he went on to write in his Report to the 1714 Committee, 'But, by reason of the motion of the ship, the variation of heat and cold, wet and dry, and the difference of gravity in different latitudes, such a watch has not yet been made'. The committee, it suggests, should look for a different solution.

In July of that year, the Longitude Act was passed, which would set up the Board of Longitude, who were tasked with finding an answer. It was made up of several distinguished scientists, and they were able to offer huge inducements for would-be inventors. Anyone producing a method that was able to guarantee accuracy to within half a degree of a 'great circle' would receive £20,000, worth over £2 million today. Methods that produced accuracy to 2 or 3 degrees would get £15,000 and to 1 degree, £10,000. This was the prize that John Harrison, the subject of this chapter, hoped to win.

Harrison was born on 24 March 1693 in the hamlet of Foulby, near Wakefield, and his father worked as a carpenter for the Wynne family at their home in Nostell Priory – this was not the magnificent Palladian mansion of today, but an earlier, more modest manor house created from some of the former monastic buildings. When the boy was quite young, probably around 1700, the family moved to the village of Barrow-upon-Humber, just across the river from the busy port of Hull. Not a great deal is known about his childhood years, but he was clearly both literate and musical. He learned to play the viol and would eventually become the choirmaster at the local church. As a teenager, he was given a copy of lectures presented by the blind mathematician Nicholas Saunderson, and his copy is covered with his own notes. Saunderson was an avid supporter of Newtonian physics and wrote about new ideas in mathematics, including the use of logarithms and differential calculus.

Harrison was to unite his love of music and mathematics later in life, when he began working on what he considered to be an improved musical scale. In traditional Western music, the top note of an octave, such as middle C to top C, should have twice the frequency of the lower notes. In between, come the tones and semitones, but not in a regular fashion – you can

Portrait of John Harrison in an engraving by Thomas Kay, 1786.
(SMG Collections CCA SA 4.0 via Wikimedia Commons)

see that by looking at the white and black notes on a piano keyboard. Harrison proposed a new scale based on logarithms and imagined the notes spread round a circle, with the ratio based on logarithms and the value of pi – the ratio between the radius and circumference of a circle. It was never widely adopted, but it is worth mentioning here as it is an example of how deeply he had studied mathematical ratios – a subject that would be essential in his later, greater work.

Because we know so little of Harrison's early years, we can only speculate based on what we know about his later life. What does seem clear is that from an early age, despite a lack of formal education, he was able to master mathematical texts intended for university students. It was perhaps this appreciation of ratios and complex relationships that decided him to turn to clock-making, even though all his early training was in woodwork.

He constructed his first clock in 1713. In many ways, it was a typical long-case pendulum clock of its time. What makes it more remarkable is that the clock mechanism was almost entirely constructed out of wood. It demonstrates his craftsmanship as a carpenter and this iconic timepiece is now on display at the Science Museum in London. The family still seems to have kept its connection with Nostell Priory and the clock he made for them is still there, with Harrison's name clearly inscribed at the foot of the dial.

His early clocks may have been similar in workings to others of the time, but he was soon making improvements of his own. He introduced the grasshopper escapement. The escapement in a pendulum clock consists of a rotating, toothed wheel, which is kept moving by means of falling weights. It periodically engages with a toothed device that moves with the swing of the pendulum, which allows the tooth to engage and disengage – escape, hence the name. This movement controls the movement of the hands. Harrison introduced his escapement, which has a complex of levers, looking rather like a grasshopper's legs.

He also worked at solving a problem that affected a metal clock pendulum: it contracted in the cold and expanded with heat, altering the swing and thus the timing. His answer was to make a grid pendulum, using metal rods of steel and brass. They expanded at different rates, so one could compensate for the other. He carried out a series of experiments to find the perfect balance. He used two identical mechanisms, placing one clock in a cold room, the other in a hot one, and set them to the same time. Once the two clocks were in perfect agreement, that was the right proportion. He had solved one of the objections Newton had to using a clock at sea – the effects of heat and cold.

Harrison was on his way to thinking about the longitude problem. But it would take time for him to even contemplate working on it.

His private life during the period he was developing his clockmaking skills was touched by tragedy. He had married Elizabeth Barrel in 1718 and had a son, John, but Elizabeth became ill and died in the spring of 1726. Just six months later he remarried, to Elizabeth Scott, and they had two children, William, born 1728, and Elizabeth, 1732.

We have moved on in time since the passing of the Longitude Act, so let's find out what had been happening in those years.

The short answer is not very much at all. There was no shortage of suggestions from the public nor from the scientific community, none of which was the least bit practical. One bizarre suggestion for keeping time was to train a dog to bark for food at the same time every day, no matter which time zone was involved. There were attempts to make clocks that could survive all the hazards outlined by Newton, but none that succeeded until Harrison began to work on the problem.

Scientists were in general sceptical about the idea of having an accurate clock and preferred a method first suggested in the early sixteenth century by the German astronomer Johannes Werner. He noticed that the Moon appeared to move across the sky at a regular rate, completing the circuit in 27.3 days – roughly speaking, its own diameter in one hour. He proposed that if at any time the angle between the Moon and some known star, such as Polaris or the Sun, was measured and the angle compared with that of the known angle taken from a different place, then the difference between the two could be used to calculate the east–west difference, hence, the longitude.

Werner was quite correct, but the method relied on an almanac being available, giving the angles from the known reference place, and no such almanac existed. It also required an accurate instrument for measuring the angle and the instruments then available were far too inaccurate.

The latter problem was originally solved by Newton, who devised an instrument in which the observer could measure the height of the celestial object above the horizon. The light reached the eyepiece via mirrors, which effectively doubled the angle, so that a quarter-turn on the instrument became an eighth of a circle, hence the name 'octant'. Newton showed his idea to John Hadley, but it was not published until after Newton's death and has become known as 'Hadley's octant'. The problem of creating a satisfactory lunar almanac had to wait a bit longer.

Charles II was apparently told by his French mistress about a method devised in France for determining longitude that had many elements in common with Werner's proposal and also required some form of almanac to give the positions of celestial bodies. The king was sufficiently impressed to agree to a suggestion from a young astronomer, John Flamsteed, to set up an observatory at Greenwich from which a team of astronomers could make and record all the necessary measurements.

Flamsteed was put in charge as the first Astronomer Royal. He began working on his star charts, using the longitude at the observatory as his base, which would eventually result in the establishment of the Greenwich meridian as zero longitude and the time set at that point would be Greenwich Mean Time (GMT). He recognised that when his work was complete, it would form the basis for a satisfactory method of finding longitude by lunar distance.

The scientific establishment of the eighteenth century was very much in favour of the lunar method for finding longitude, though there were several problems involved in its use, not least the fact that it required complex calculations to get a result. There was, there is no doubt, a certain prejudice attached to the idea that an uneducated craftsman could find a better solution – a problem that was to plague Harrison in his dealings with the Longitude Board.

Harrison began working on the accuracy of clocks with the help of his younger brother, James, using clocks based on the gridiron pendulum and grasshopper escapement. They were aware that the only test of accuracy was the observation of the stars. Because of the rotation of the earth, the position of the stars would change by three minutes and fifty-six seconds in any twenty-four-hour period. They used their own rather crude instrument to measure time over a period of a month and found the clocks worked to within one second of the celestial time. At some point during these experiments, Harrison realised that he might be on the way to solving the longitude problem. But he was also aware that a pendulum clock could never keep accurate time on a ship that was bobbing around on the ocean waves. He would need to devise a new mechanism and began to prepare drawings of how it would work.

In 1830, he went to London in the hope of presenting his designs to the Longitude Board, but he was thwarted by the simple fact that there was no official meeting place for the members for the very good reason that none of the proposals sent in over the years had been worth discussing, so they had never met. He was, however, aware that the Royal Observatory existed and he went there, where he was received by Flamsteed's successor, John Hadley. The astronomer suggested that Harrison, instead of going straight to the board members, should first get the approval of his design from a leading London clockmaker, George Graham. The latter was so impressed by the design that he gave Harrison a substantial loan to help him build an actual clock, which could be tested.

Harrison returned to Barrow and began work on what would be known as H1. It took him five years. The clock has survived and looks unlike any other timepiece of the time. The pendulum mechanism of the long clocks has gone and to ensure the clock was not affected by the swaying of a ship, Harrison used compensating swinging balances and helical springs. He was probably aware that if he was going to impress sophisticated Londoners, it would have to look the part, so in the fashion of the time, it had elaborate decoration – and might originally have had an outer case, but that has never been found. It was originally put on show at Graham's workshops and Graham himself wrote to the Longitude Board recommending it – 'it highly deserves Public Encouragement'.

The board agreed to set up sea trials, but showed little enthusiasm for the project and a whole year went by before Harrison was finally taken, with his clock, to Spithead to join a naval vessel bound for Portugal in 1736. The clock fared better than Harrison, who was violently seasick throughout the voyage. When they reached port, the captain was taken ill and died, and the new captain, Roger Wills, received orders to return at once to England.

On the return voyage, Wills placed the ship as being on the approach to Dartmouth, but Harrison trusted the clock and declared they were actually miles away, close to the Lizard. He was right, and Wills duly reported the fact. It was a very practical demonstration of the value of the timepiece, and when Harrison was interviewed by the board, they were suitably impressed. He had, they declared, succeeded in making a timepiece that met the basic conditions of the Longitude Act, but Harrison was a perfectionist, and simply asked for funds to enable him to work on a much better version.

The board agreed to provide £500 for developing the new version, H2, of which £250 was to be supplied immediately and the rest when it passed a suitable trial. They also required that Harrison presented the clock to the board together with H1. The new clock might have been an improvement, but Harrison was still not happy, so it was never given a sea trial.

H3 was to occupy Harrison for another nineteen years, during which time he received more grants, but had to fit in working on the new device with the ordinary work of a local clockmaker, on which his income still relied. He did, however, receive a significant honour during that time, being awarded the Copley Gold Medal by the Royal Society for his outstanding contribution to science.

The problem with all these clocks was their complexity. H3 had an astonishing 753 components. He had continued to use the gridiron idea that he had first developed for his pendulum clocks to compensate for temperature changes. But in this third clock, he used the far smaller bimetal strip, consisting of two metals bound together, each with a different rate of expansion when heated, a device he is generally credited with inventing. He also incorporated ball bearings for the first time to ensure smooth movements.

He was still not satisfied, but in 1753 he had a pocket watch made for his personal use by a London watchmaker, John Jefferys. It seems to have been mainly, if not altogether, based on Harrison's own design, and included a bimetallic strip and kept excellent time. At a meeting of the Longitude Board in

The time ball above the Greenwich Royal Observatory was raised then dropped at a precise time, which allowed seamen in ships on the Thames to set their chronometers. (Peter Whatley, CCA SA 2.0 via Wikimedia Commons)

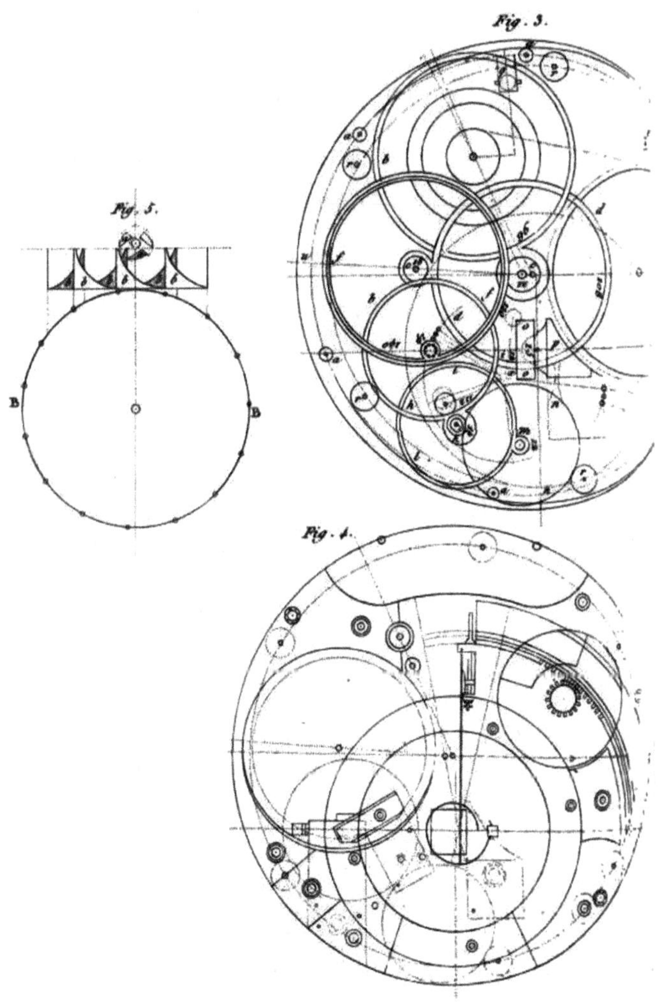

The mechanism of Harrison's H4 chronometer from *The Principles of Mr. Harrison's Time-keeper* (1767).

London, Harrison suggested that such a small machine might well be useful 'with respect to longitude'. It was the starting point for developing H4.

H4 is large by the standard of modern watches, at 5in diameter, but tiny compared with its predecessors. Like modern watches, it used jewelled movements to replace the complexities of the visible movements of his first clocks. Now, at last, he was satisfied that he had a timepiece worthy of the Longitude prize.

It was originally intended that H3 and H4 should both be given a sea trial, but the departure date for the ship was endlessly delayed. Dava Sobel, in her book *Longitude* (1995), suggests that this might have been a deliberate delaying tactic inaugurated by Nevil Maskelyne, the new Astronomer Royal, and an enthusiastic supporter of the lunar method. History is, however, littered with accounts of the Admiralty dithering over the acceptance of new ideas.

Eventually, just H4 was to be tried, and it was placed aboard HMS *Deptford* for a voyage to the West Indies. William Harrison went in place of his now elderly father. They finally departed for the West Indies, but once at sea, a disastrous discovery was made – all the beer on board had gone off and had to be jettisoned and the crew were reduced to drinking water. Now history repeated itself: once again, the captain and his officers, using traditional navigational skills, placed the ship in one place, while William and the watch gave a quite different reading. According to William, they would soon see Madeira and could take on fresh supplies, and sure enough, it came into sight the following morning. Captain Digger at once declared that when back in Britain, he would buy a timekeeper like it from the Harrisons.

The return to Britain was a nightmare for William, with heavy seas threatening to swamp the clock and himself feverish and seasick. But on reaching port, the result seemed to be worth all the effort, for the total time difference was still just two minutes.

The Harrisons very reasonably expected the board to approve the trial and award them the prize, but they had not allowed for just how wedded they, and Maskelyne in particular, were to the lunar method. They demanded that three mathematicians be appointed to check all the measurements made by the astronomers. They decided that although they had themselves appointed those responsible, they were not sufficiently accurate. H4 may have performed brilliantly, but it could have been a one-off performance. There would have to be a second trial.

Once again, William had to undergo a sea voyage to the West Indies and arrived only to find that the astronomer appointed to check the accuracy was none other than their chief opponent, Nevil Maskelyne. Despite that, the trial once again showed that H4 had accurately kept time and correctly measured longitude. There was no longer any doubt.

Now, however, new obstacles were put in the way. To prove it could be reproduced, Harrison was required to take H4 to pieces and reassemble it in the presence of experts. He was required to make two more watches and hand over all the specifications so that another competent watchmaker could reproduce it.

The duplicate, known as K1, was used by Captain Cook on his second round-the-world voyage. It was found to be perfectly accurate and ideal for quickly determining longitude – where the best and most proficient navigators required at least four hours to produce the same result using the lunar method.

It was clear that Harrison had met every condition laid down by the Longitude Board, even though they changed them all the time, but there was still no sign of receiving the prize money. Eventually, an appeal was made to Parliament and an award of £8,750 was made to Harrison, but he was never to receive the honour of being acknowledged by the Longitude Board – the prize was never, in fact, to be awarded.

Harrison died in 1776, and though he never received the prize he had spent so many years pursuing, he did live long enough to see that, although it was K1 and not his own H4, the watch he had designed had proved its worth on Cook's voyage. After his death, whatever the Board of Longitude might have thought, mariners and watchmakers appreciated the value of what he had done and the manufacture of marine chronometers began to gain momentum.

The lunar method continued in use, and in 1767, Greenwich published the first nautical almanac, providing information on the position of the Moon in respect to other heavenly bodies. In later years, the almanac became more detailed, with information on the position of many stars and planets. It is still published annually.

Harrison's legacy lives on. In the 1950s, I was called up for National Service and was fortunate enough to be accepted for training as a navigator in the RAF. The navigational techniques and instruments I used then were not really very different from those used by the sailors of the eighteenth century. My normal wristwatch was replaced by a more accurate one set to Greenwich Mean Time. I had the use of a sextant – the successor to the octant – with which I could measure the angle of any recognisable heavenly body above the horizon, and a copy of the nautical almanac for that year. With these I could not merely discover the longitude, but by taking a succession of readings of two, or better still, three, different celestial bodies, I could calculate very quickly exactly where the plane was at a particular time. If the point fell on the

Ship's officers checking their position using sextants.

course plotted on the chart at take-off, then everything was in order – if not, a new course had to be plotted, and a new compass bearing passed to the pilot. None of this, however, would have been possible without an accurate timekeeper that kept me and generations of navigators before me on course to our destination.

Although Harrison did eventually receive the recognition he deserved for his work on the chronometer, that was not his whole life. His love of music remained with him, and he would no doubt be surprised to hear that over two centuries later, he would be the subject for a musical work celebrating his achievement – *Harrison's Clocks*. He would, however, have found Harrison Birtwistle's music quite unlike anything he had ever heard before.

2

PIERRE-PAUL RIQUET

*The developer of the Canal du Midi, which was the
first canal to cross a watershed and featured locks,
aqueducts and the first canal tunnel.*

In this chapter, we are moving away from the oceans of the
world to the inland waterways of Europe. Canals were not
exactly new in the seventeenth century. Records show that
the pharaoh Pepi I, who ruled from 2332–2283 BCE, ordered
five canals to be constructed to carry stone for the building of
the Men-Nefer-Pepi pyramid. The name means 'Pepi's splen-
dour lives forever', but the pyramid today is little more than
a pile of rubble.

There was no real problem in building canals over level
ground, but rises and falls had to be overcome by the construction of locks. These seem first to have been used in
China over 2,000 years ago, but they were much slower
to develop in Europe. The first locks were known as flash
locks and were introduced on rivers. Weirs were built with
gates with removable sections. Water accumulated upstream
and when boats needed to pass, the removable sections were

taken out, and the gate opened, allowing the boats going downstream to ride the rushing water, known as 'the flash' – hence the name flash lock. Boats going upstream generally had to be winched against the flow.

However, such devices were of no use on the still waters of canals, so the 'pound lock' was introduced, with a chamber that was closed by gates at both ends. A boat going up the canal would enter the empty chamber, the gate closed behind it and water from the upper level let in to raise the boat until it reached the appropriate level, at which point the top gate could be opened and the vessel continued on its way. The process was reversed for boats travelling in the opposite direction.

In the earliest version, the gates were lifted vertically in a frame via a winch. This was cumbersome and, when wide locks were needed, difficult to operate. Using a conventional gate presented a difficulty – it was hard to move. Dividing the gate into two sections only created a fresh problem as the force of water tended to push the two sections apart.

This was solved in the fifteenth century by the extraordinary genius, Leonardo da Vinci, who invented the mitre gate for a canal in Milan. The two gates were designed to meet at an angle, so that water pressure pushed them closer together – this is the system used on all modern canals. His original sketch has survived in the *Codex Atlanticus*, which is now held in the Ambrosiana Library in Milan. Canal construction was entering a new age.

Plans for major canal construction in France began at the end of the sixteenth century with a proposal that would link the rivers Loire and Seine, but there were major surveying errors and the first proposed solution proved to be totally impractical. New ideas were brought forward, and in 1604, work began on what would become the Canal de Briare, linking Briare on the Loire to Rogny on the River Loing, a navigable tributary of the Seine. There were some notable engineering features, one being at Rogny itself, where the canal arrived high above river level. The two waterways were joined by a staircase of seven locks, not separate, but all linked together, so that the bottom gate of the top lock was also the top lock of the one below and so on. The canal was a success, and brought forward ideas for an even more ambitious scheme, one that would not just unite rivers, but seas – joining the Mediterranean to the Atlantic.

The idea was for a canal that would create the link from the River Garonne, which was navigable from the coast to Bordeaux, by canal to Toulouse and from there down the River Saude to the Mediterranean. As with the Briare, early plans proved impractical. No engineer could come up with a solution to the major problem that this was a 'summit' canal, which simply means that it would rise from one river valley and then eventually drop back down to the next. This would involve locks at both ends. So, if one pictures a boat setting off on a journey through the whole system, it would start by entering the first lock. Water would come in from the upper level and eventually the boat would move on up through the locks until it reached the top, and the water for the final lock would come from the summit level of the canal. Going down the other side, it would enter a full lock, and the water from that would also come from the summit and flow on down.

Altogether, each boat passing along the canal would drain two locks' worth of water from the summit. Unless that water could be replaced, the summit would rapidly run dry. And that was the snag. The summit of the proposed canal passed through a notably arid region, and no one could think up a way of fixing the problem – and that is where Pierre-Paul Riquet enters the story.

A portrait engraving of Pierre-Paul Riquet.

Riquet was born at Béziers in 1609, although there has been some dispute about the date, with some placing it earlier. His father was a lawyer and businessman, wealthy and influential. As a teenager, Riquet's main interests were in the sciences and mathematics, studies that would later be put to good use. He was married at the age of 18 to a wealthy heiress, Catherine de Milhau.

In 1630, thanks to family interest, he was appointed to the post of collector of the salt tax, the *gabelle*, for Languedoc-Roussillon. This was a hugely unpopular tax, which was inescapable, as everyone over a certain age was required to buy a minimum amount of salt each year, usually 8kg, at a price set by the government which included the tax. Rates varied for different regions and the job of collecting the taxes was farmed out. Riquet received a commission for his share in this highly profitable government, which remained in use until the French Revolution.

He also had another business, in collaboration with his brother-in-law, as an arms dealer, supplying weapons to the Catalan Army. By the time he was 50, he was wealthy enough to retire to his country chateau, Bonrepos, near Toulouse. But instead of settling down to a quiet life, he began taking an interest in the old idea of the canal to join the two seas.

Riquet knew the Languedoc region well from his extensive travels and was aware of the value a canal would be to the region. This was very much his country. His first language was the local language, Occitan, and in a letter he wrote to the king's chief minister, he apologised for not writing very clearly, admitting that he was not scholarly, had no Latin or Greek, and his French was not particularly good either. It seems, in fact, that he had to employ someone else to compose the letter in French.

He was sure that he could, with his intimate knowledge of the region, find an answer to the problem of water supply. He was sufficiently practical, however, to realise that he would need the help of a qualified engineer. He discussed the matter with a friend, the Bishop of Castres, Monsignor d'Anglure de Bourlemont, who recommended a young man, François Andréossy.

Andréossy was born in Paris in 1633 and studied engineering there. In 1660, he went to Italy, touring Padua and Lombardy to inspect the canal works there, so he was well suited to provide Riquet with practical experience. General Andréossy wrote a history of the canal in 1804, in which he claimed that his great-grandson should be considered the real person to get the credit for the scheme. There is a case for saying this, but it was Riquet's vision that made the whole scheme possible – and had things gone badly wrong, it was Riquet who would have taken the blame. He was very much the man in charge, but that does not mean that one should not acknowledge the young man's immense and essential contribution to the project.

Riquet discovered that the River Sor, which emerged from the Montagne Noire, was at a height of 16.5m above the proposed summit level of the canal. Nearly some 1,500 paces away was a brook, the Lampy, as well as other brooks. By uniting them, he believed that they could supply enough water to feed a canal that was 16.5m wide and 1.8m deep with locks. These would not only take river barges, but also merchant ships, who could avoid the long and sometimes dangerous journey through the straits at Gibraltar. This was not just speculation: he had carried out a whole series of hydraulic experiments at his chateau, to work out water flows. He now needed official permission for the actual construction.

Once again, he was helped by his friend, de Bourlemont, who was now the Archbishop of Toulouse. He suggested contacting the chief minister, Jean-Baptiste Colbert. He was a powerful figure in the government and was an enthusiastic economic reformer, who rooted out a great deal of corruption and was a keen promoter of trade. The scheme was one that appealed to his plans for modernising the French economy.

Riquet and the archbishop were invited to meet Colbert in Paris, and he sent his private coach for them. Everything went well and Colbert agreed to discuss the proposal with King Louis XIV, who approved the setting up of a royal commission to look at the proposal and report on its viability.

It seems that only one member of the commission had any practical experience or knowledge of engineering, and that was Henri de Boutheroue, whose father had been the chief engineer during the construction of the Briare Canal. By now, Riquet had had more thoughts about the route the canal would take. Earlier versions had terminated at Carcassonne, but now it was intended to extend it all the way to the Mediterranean at Étang de Thau, where a new port would be developed and was to be called Cette (now Sète). The water-supply system had initially been envisaged as a whole string of reservoirs, feeding down through several channels, known as *rigoles*. This was now to be simplified to just two *rigoles* – the Rigole de la Montagne, which would start high in the mountains and run for 24km to meet the main *rigole*, the Rigole de la Plaine, which ran a further 34km to reach the canal summit level at Col de Naurouze. They would be fed partly by natural springs, but the main supply would come from a reservoir created by building a dam across the River Laudot at Saint-Ferréol.

As many engineers have discovered over the years, the problems of construction are comparatively simple compared to getting a committee to make up its collective mind. One sticking point was the Rigole de la Montagne, which they thought could not succeed. At this point, Riquet stepped in with a proposal that he would personally pay for a survey to prove its feasibility. Not surprisingly, they agreed.

After a year's delay, he was able to make a start, but he had still not received authorisation to build the canal itself. There was yet more argument, this time over who should pay for what, and it was decided that answering that question should be the work of yet another committee. Eventually, agreement was reached: the Province of Languedoc would be authorised to use the salt tax to pay for construction of the canal, and Riquet and his successors would be allowed to take the tolls charged for using the waterway.

In October 1666, four years after the first meeting with Colbert, the king authorised construction that was expected to take eight years to complete and was to cost 3,360,000 livres, over 17 million euros at today's prices.

Building the dam was a huge project – it was the biggest in Europe at the time. Saint-Ferréol had been chosen because the riverbed at that point was solid granite, an ideal foundation. There were to be three granite walls, infilled by a mixture of rubble and clay. Inside the walls there were galleries providing access to the valves that controlled the flow of water and a tunnel at the base, colourfully known as the 'entrance to hell'.

A contemporary engraving showing the profile of Saint-Ferréol Dam.

Work got under way in 1667, and the workforce consisted of around 12,000 'heads' – not the same as 12,000 people. Each man counted as a single head, but three women became just two heads. The women had an important and arduous role to play. This was a wild region with no decent roads, so one of their jobs was to bring stone from the quarries in wicker baskets.

When completed in 1680, it was an immense curved structure, 780m long at the top and with a base with a maximum width of 140m. When the reservoir behind it filled, it held around 680,000 cubic metres of water, which was considered more than enough to ensure that the summit level of the canal never ran dry, no matter how much traffic it carried.

Riquet was extremely proud of the work, and he planted trees on the slope beside the dam. Overflow water was allowed to fall through a series of cascades, while some came down a pipe to feed an imposing fountain at the bottom. No one except an engineer could call the great stone wall of the dam a thing of beauty, but the grounds and water features have helped make it something of a tourist attraction.

Work on the *rigoles* had started much earlier in 1665, and they may not seem quite so dramatic as the dam, but careful planning went into designing those as well. Riquet's plan called for them to follow natural contours, with a very gentle slope to give a smooth flow. Even so, there was considerable work involved, and the job of supervising the levels was overseen by Andréossy.

The work included a tunnel, 122m long and 3m wide. The *rigoles* had generous dimensions, originally 6m wide with a depth of 1.8m, but Riquet decided to widen some sections to allow them to be used by small boats to carry construction material for the canal-builders. The *rigole* system reached the canal at Naurouze, where a large basin was constricted. Riquet had hoped that a whole new town would develop there and that the basin would be lined with warehouses. The centre-piece of this new settlement would be an immensely elaborate statue of Louis XIV in a chariot being pulled by seahorses, a drawing of which exists – but that is as far as it and the town ever got. For a while, there were attempts to run boats on the *rigole*, but they never prospered.

When work on the canal itself began, it was organised into twelve divisions, each with its own supervisor. When the first five deep locks were built at the Toulouse end of the canal, they were entirely conventional with vertical walls. However, one of them collapsed inward and Riquet decided to redesign the chambers. On the new locks, the walls were curved, so that the chamber was oval-shaped. The new walls now had the strength associated with the arch form.

The canal not only had single lock chambers, but many multiples – nineteen double staircases, four triple, one quadruple and one sextuple. Altogether, a boat travelling the whole 240km route would have to pass through ninety-nine lock chambers. These were all large, 30m by 5.5m minimum.

One strange lock was built at Agde, where there was a problem with boats travelling between the River Hérault and the canal, the port being at a different level. A boat wanting to leave the canal would have to turn through 90 degrees, which would have been extremely difficult. The answer was to have a circular lock in which a boat could be swung and then either continue on the canal or join the river.

Inevitably, there were rivers to be crossed along the way, most of which were originally crossed on the level. There have been many changes to the canal over the years, and only one aqueduct built in Riquet's time survives, at Répudre, a solidly built single stone arch. The Cesse crossing was originally made possible by the construction of a dam across the river

One of the *rigoles* that carried water from the reservoir at Saint-Ferréol to the summit of the Canal du Midi. (Author)

An aerial view of one of the typical oval locks on the Canal du Midi crowded with pleasure boats. (Author)

to equalise water levels. Shortly after the canal was opened, this was demolished and replaced by a three-arched aqueduct.

Inevitably, in such a long route, the different ground met along the way required different construction measures. In places the channel had to be driven through hard rock, which had to be blasted away with gunpowder. This was highly labour intensive, since holes for the powder had to be drilled by hand. In other places, the ground was porous, and the canal had to be made watertight. It had to be puddled, which involved making a semi-fluid mixture of clay and water, then stamping it into the ground, layer upon layer, until it dried to a complete seal.

The technical difficulties of canal construction were not the only things to slow progress. There were constant worries about finance, which ultimately depended on collecting the salt tax. As mentioned earlier, this was deeply unpopular and the tax collectors shared in the unpopularity. At one point, Riquet wrote a letter to Colbert in which he remarked they were working in a region in which murder was as common as bread and wine. The tax collectors always went armed – and were quite prepared to kill any attackers.

It had originally been expected that the whole work would be completed in eight years – it became clear that this was not going to happen. The people on the ground knew that they were moving as fast as possible and understood why things did not always go well. Officials in Paris, however, were becoming increasingly exasperated, and there was talk of bringing in new men to run the project. Riquet received news of this just as he was about to tackle a problem that was entirely new to canal construction – he needed to build a tunnel under a hill at the aptly named Malpas – 'bed step'. The commissioners were about to descend on the works, and if they were not satisfied, then changes would be made.

The Malpas Tunnel, carved through solid rock. (Martonvl, CCA SA 4.0 via Wikimedia Commons)

Riquet was always an astute man, and he realised that if there was anything likely to impress them then it would be the sight of work completed on the first ever canal tunnel. He called in every available man working in the area to the tunnel. They were set to work hacking through the comparatively soft sandstone, while teams of carpenters followed behind, shoring up the roof, and masons lined the sides. Although the tunnel is just 165m long, it is over 7m wide and the crown of the roof is 5.8m above the waterline. It is said that the work was completed in six days to be ready for the commissioners' visit – if so, then preliminary work must have already been under way when Riquet got the message.

Visiting the tunnel, it presents an odd, unfinished face. The western end has a handsome stone portal, but at the opposite end, there is just the natural rock, so that it looks like the entrance to a grotto. Perhaps Riquet had managed to get one end completed and suitably impressive by the time the visitors arrived, after which it had done its job and the workforce moved on. Whatever the reason, Riquet had won a reprieve and was able to continue in charge.

The last great obstacle to overcome was the connection to the River Orb, and Riquet's critics declared that the ground was simply too steep and the canal would never reach it. Once again, Riquet confounded his critics by designing the great eight-lock staircase at Fonseranes, which was to take the canal down to a crossing of the River Orb with a total fall of 21.5m over 300m.

With that done, the work was almost over, but Riquet did not live to see it completed. He died in October 1680 at the age of 76.

The opening ceremony took place on what was now known as the Canal Royal en Languedoc – later shortened to the more manageable Canal du Midi – on 15 May 1681. A fleet of boats set off from the Garonne, reaching Cette ten days later.

The canal was to be a great success financially, and eventually there would be around 259 vessels regularly trading on the waterway. As well as cargo boats, there were regular mail boats that began taking passengers from 1684, with up to 30,000 using the service. In 1776, La Nouvelle branch was constructed, running from the Canal du Midi for 37km through Narbonne to Port-la-Nouvelle.

By the middle of the nineteenth century, traffic had peaked at 110 million tonnes-km per annum. However, some parts of the original system were proving inadequate, in particular, the often-difficult crossing of the Orb at Béziers, where at one time, traffic was held up for over a fortnight by flood water. In 1858, the problem was solved by the construction of a 240m-long aqueduct that connected to the Fonseranes Staircase, making the bottom two locks redundant. Other major works improved the efficiency of the navigation.

The twentieth century saw serious competition from road traffic. Other French waterways had introduced new barges, the 38.5m-long *péniches* with a cargo capacity of 250 tonnes. The Canal du Midi locks had been more than adequate for the trade of the seventeenth century, but were unable to take the new vessels, so in the late 1970s work began on extending the locks to meet the new demand.

An even more ambitious project was put in place in the 1980s to bypass the Fonseranes Staircase with a water slope. The vessels were floated into a wedge of water that was held back by a movable gate. The gate was taken up and down the slope by locomotives on tracks beside the slope, carrying the wedge of water and the craft with them. However,

The eight-lock staircase at Fonseranes, which lifts the canal a total of 21.5m. (Tournasol7, CCA SA 3.0 via Wikimedia Commons)

there were problems with the mechanism and the slope was abandoned.

Despite the improvements, cargo-carrying on the canal continued to diminish but it was to continue in use for the increasingly popular holiday traffic. Today, the waterway is busy with private, hired and hotel boats, most of the latter being converted barges. Riquet would no doubt be astonished by the craft using his waterway, but delighted to find it still in use over two centuries after he first dreamed of the scheme. But the canal also played a part in the development of canals in Britain.

Francis Egerton was born in 1736 and was never supposed to inherit the family title of Duke of Bridgewater, as he was the youngest of five children, but the brothers all died, and he became the 3rd Duke at the age of just 12. He had always been a sickly child and was considered not very bright, and as a result, his education had been rather neglected. Now he had to catch up and in his late teens he had to undertake the right of passage of all young aristocrats – the Grand Tour of Europe.

He set off with his tutor, starting in Paris, where he was unimpressed by the theatrical performance he attended, but took an enthusiastic interest in 'actresses' – young ladies whose performances did most certainly not take place in public. He was hastily moved on to Italy, where he did the conventional thing of collecting antiquities, which were crated up and sent to his home at Worsley, near Manchester. It is said they were never opened until after his death. But if he was not interested in antiquities, he was greatly impressed by the Canal du Midi.

On his return to England, the duke had a brief period in London, which ended when he had a disastrous love affair. He retired to his estates, which included the extensive Worsley coal mines. He was aware that his profits could be greatly increased by having easy access to the rapidly growing demand

The barge *Alathilde*, adapted as a hotel boat on the Canal du Midi. (Neil Crawford)

in Manchester. He began to plan for a canal that would link the mines to the nearby Irwell Navigation, but the navigation authorities refused to co-operate. The duke, however, had seen in France that canals could be taken across rivers on aqueducts and the new plan was a direct link to Manchester via an aqueduct over the Irwell at Barton.

He had the help of his agent, John Gilbert, and a former millwright, James Brindley, in constructing the canal. It is a mark of the insularity of some engineers at the time that one of them remarked, when hearing of the proposed aqueduct, that he had heard of castles in the air, but had never thought of anyone being silly enough to try to build one. It was, however, built and the canal was opened in 1761. It was a commercial success and was soon extended to join the River Mersey at Runcorn, via a flight of locks designed to take Mersey barges, roughly 70ft long and 14ft beam.

The success of the Bridgewater Canal caused a surge of interest and soon new schemes were being put forward, including a canal system that would link four major rivers, the Trent, Mersey, Thames and Severn. James Brindley was the leading figure.

He might have been expected to continue building locks to the same dimensions as those at Runcorn but on the Trent & Mersey Canal he was faced with hills at Harecastle that were impossible to go around and the only alternative was a tunnel – although it would need to be almost 3,000 yards long. He baulked at the idea of making it big enough to take 14ft-wide barges, so he decided to halve its width.

Riquet had faced a far less difficult situation at Malpas and even if the work wasn't completed in six days, it was comparatively quick. Harecastle Tunnel was to take eleven years to complete, so Brindley was probably wise not to attempt anything grander. As a result of that decision, however, Brindley decided that as no boat wider than 7ft could get through the tunnel, there was no point in making locks any wider either. The result was that throughout a large part of the British canal system, cargo was carried in narrowboats. Although the British system developed a century after Riquet began work on his great masterwork, the carrying capacity was nowhere near as large.

Riquet's Canal du Midi had all the features that were to appear on later canals: locks, both single and in staircases, aqueducts and a tunnel, but its most striking feature remains the great dam and the *rigoles* that made the summit canal possible. On visiting the canal a few years ago, I found there was much to impress, especially the Fonseranes Staircase of locks, but nothing came close to the grandeur of the great dam at St Ferréol. Riquet's achievements were recognised in 1666, when Louis XIV awarded him the title of Baron of Bonrepos, and a splendid statue of him can be seen in Toulouse, but his greatest monument remains the canal that linked two seas.

3

JOSEPH-MICHEL AND JACQUES-ÉTIENNE MONTGOLFIER

The inventors of the hot-air balloon, the world's first practical device that enabled human beings to fly.

Mankind has, it seems, always dreamed of emulating the birds and taking to the skies. Flying men appear in legends in many different cultures, from the unhappy Icarus who flew too close to the sun, where his wings fell off, to ancient Sanskrit documents found in India in the nineteenth century in which there are accounts of amazing flying machines.

The first recorded attempt to fly dates to the first century CE, when the Chinese Emperor Wang Mang had a set of wings made and ordered one of his servants to put them on and jump off the top of a tower. Energetic flapping made no impression, and he landed just 100 yards from the base of the tower. It was the first of several attempts to fly with artificial wings.

The nearest to a successful flight appears to have taken place in the ninth century at Cordova, then part of Moorish Spain, when Abbas Ibn Firnas claimed to have stayed aloft for an impressive ten minutes, but no details of exactly how he achieved this have survived. Although the flight was a success, his landing was not – he injured his back and never repeated the experiment.

In Britain, William of Malmesbury wrote an account of a young monk who was impressed by watching jackdaws circling overhead, built himself a pair of wings and in 1010 leapt off a tower, only to crash and break both his legs. He wanted to try again, this time adding a tail to his wings, but the abbot wisely vetoed the plan.

As late as 1517, attempts were still being made with artificial wings, when John Damian launched himself from the top of Stirling Castle with predictable results. He claimed afterwards that he would have succeeded had he used eagle feathers instead of chicken feathers for his wings – but wisely, he never put that theory to the test.

We now know that all attempts to fly with flapping wings are doomed – the best one can hope for is to glide smoothly down without flapping. The problem that remained was not how to make the descent safely, but how to rise from the ground.

There were various attempts to devise flying machines. Most famously by Leonardo da Vinci, who produced a design for a form of helicopter, but like all such attempts, it was doomed to fail for lack of a power source. The truth is that *Homo sapiens*, as a species, do not have the muscular ability to imitate the birds.

There was an answer available, however, as early as the third century BCE. The Chinese produced flying lanterns in which a small lamp was placed below a paper balloon and as the air in the balloon warmed up it took to the air. Chinese lanterns are still sometimes used today. The same idea finally reached Europe when a priest, Bartolomeu de Gusmão, demonstrated his version of a Chinese lantern to the Lisbon court in 1709. No one, however, seems to have thought that the idea might be scaled up to take human beings into the air until the end of the eighteenth century when two brothers made aviation history, Joseph-Michel and Jacques-Étienne Montgolfier.

The Montgolfier family had a long tradition of papermaking. The process originated in the Far East and travelled across to the Middle East and paper mills were established in Damascus. One of the earlier Montgolfiers was captured while fighting in the Sixth Crusade. During his time in imprisonment, he learnt the technology, and on his return to France in 1386, he established a paper mill in the Auvergne region of France. By the eighteenth century, they had established a number of mills at Annonay, in the Ardeche.

Pierre and Anne Montgolfier had fifteen children: Joseph-Michel was the twelfth, born in 1740, and Jacques-Étienne was the fifteenth, born in 1745. The family business was passed to the eldest son, Robert. Joseph-Michel was said to have been a bit of a dreamer and after leaving school he went to Paris, where he became interested in the latest scientific experiments including the recently discovered method of making hydrogen, which he called 'inflammable air'. He was soon called back to Annonay to help with the family business and promptly began suggesting new methods for making paper. The family were unimpressed but financed him to set up on his own — as the business rapidly failed, the decision not to let him experiment in their own successful mills seems wise. Robert died unexpectedly young and Jacques-Étienne, who had trained as an architect, took over.

Portrait of the Montgolfier brothers on a medallion by the sculptor Jean-Antoine Houdon.

Joseph became interested in the idea of flying and before he had even begun thinking of ballooning he devised an early form of parachute, which he tried out himself, jumping from the top of a building. The idea of ballooning occurred to him when contemplating the Siege of Gibraltar in 1782, when the combined forces of France and Spain were trying and failing to take the British garrison by land and sea. Would it be possible, he wondered, to take the fortress using airborne troops? This set him thinking about how this might be achieved.

It was said that while thinking about the problem, he watched embers from a fire rising up the chimney and thought that they were being carried up by the smoke. He built a small parallelpiped box frame measuring 90cm by 90cm by 120cm and covered it with taffeta, lit a fire underneath and watched it rise to the ceiling. He saw that this might be enlarged to make his hoped-for troop transporter and called for his brother, Jacques-Étienne, to join him to continue the experiments.

Their next attempt was altogether grander in scale with a volume of around 200m³. When they lit the fire underneath it, it took off out of their control and finally landed 2km away. There is evidence that Joseph also thought of using hydrogen, but it would have leaked out through the taffeta.

Following this success, the brothers decided the time was right for a public demonstration, but they made one important change. Instead of the wooden-framed construction, they replaced it with an almost-spherical balloon of sackcloth lined with thin paper, the three separate parts of the envelope buttoned together. It was the biggest version yet, with a maximum capacity of almost 800m³.

On 4 June 1783, it was flown from Annonay in front of a crowd of local dignitaries. When fully inflated, it took eight strong men to hold it down. Once they let go, it shot up like a cork from a bottle of champagne, which must have amazed the crowd on the ground – just as it surprised me on my first balloon trip. It rose to an estimated height of almost 2,000m and in a flight of around ten minutes covered just over 2km. This was not as far as expected, and Jacques-Étienne decided that it was due to air escaping through the buttonholes, which was probably the correct explanation. Nevertheless, it had flown.

The next step was obvious: demonstrate the new marvel in Paris. Joseph-Michel may have been the inventive genius behind the project, but it was Jacques-Étienne who was the more sophisticated of the two and was known for his social graces. He went alone to the capital to arrange and promote the flight.

The Montgolfiers decided that for the Paris demonstration, improvements needed to be made – no more buttonholes. As paper manufacturers, they knew this was a possible material but recognised that it would have to be of a particular type to prevent collapse and leaks, so they turned to a wallpaper manufacturer, Jean-Baptiste Réveillon, who had a factory at Faubourg St Antoine.

This was to be a massive and curiously shaped balloon, 22.5m high by 13m at the widest point. It was described as having a pyramidal top, a prismatic middle section and a truncated cone at the bottom. The fabric consisted of two layers of paper, with linen sandwiched in between. It would obviously have been a PR disaster if the official demonstration before the royal family at Versailles went wrong, so it was decided to have a trial flight in Réveillon's garden before an invited audience, including members of the Académie Française. The balloon had to be brought to the garden in sections, which were then stitched – not buttoned – together.

On 11 September 1783, everything was in place for the trial flight. A special platform was erected with a central hole into which the neck of the balloon was fitted. Underneath was a furnace to heat the air. The balloon itself was secured by a frame and ropes, and twenty men were employed to control the process of inflation, ensuring that the envelope expanded evenly, so that no cracks appeared.

At first everything went well – in just ten minutes the balloon had inflated and began a controlled lift above the heads of the crowd. The men on the ground struggled to keep it under control but managed successfully. Then disaster struck.

A sudden storm blew up, with high winds and lashing rain. The handlers did their best, but the sodden fabric made it almost impossible to control the balloon and soon the wind had begun tearing it to shreds. The balloon that was intended for triumph at Versailles was wrecked beyond repair.

The first flight of the Montgolfier balloon from Annonay.
(Library of Congress)

The Montgolfiers were faced with a dilemma. Should they inform the royal family that the grand event would have to be postponed? Unthinkable! The only solution was to make a new balloon – and there were just seven days in which to do so. The elaborate design was abandoned in favour of a conventional, slightly pear-shaped balloon of rather more modest size, with a height of 17m and a diameter of 12.5m. It was grandly embellished with decoration in blue and gold. There was just time for a short, tethered trail flight, before it was packed away and taken to Versailles.

Preparations for the display were screened off, ready for the moment when everything would be revealed. On the evening before the flight, the Montgolfier brothers were treated to a royal banquet. The next day, the courtiers gathered, waiting for Louis and Marie Antoinette to appear. The royal couple were invited to inspect the balloon before taking their places for the main event. The brothers suggested that perhaps this might be an opportunity for the first human flight, but the king vetoed the suggestion as too dangerous.

Instead of a volunteer human, the dubious honour instead went to a sheep named Montauciel – 'climb to the sky' – as a reasonable approximation to human physiology, a duck, which, because it could fly anyway, was expected to show no reaction, and a rooster, which might be alarmed at being whisked up to the skies. They were loaded into a wickerwork basket and everything was ready for the launch. Astronomers had taken up positions around the palace to observe the flight and measure the height to which the balloon rose and a barometer was added to the basket along with the livestock.

The signal to release the balloon was given by the firing of three cannon. It rose rapidly into the air and was carried away on a light breeze. Several spectators tried to follow on foot,

A tethered flight in the garden of the paper manufacturer Réveillon.

but were only able to see it disappear, slowly losing height, above the trees of the Vaucresson Forest.

The basket was located some 3km from Versailles. It was badly damaged, but not, it seems, its unwilling occupants. The sheep was placidly nibbling the grass, the duck was wandering around and only the cockerel had suffered any damage – a wing had apparently been kicked by the sheep. They did not know it, but they were the world's first aeronauts.

The day was deemed a resounding success. One of the first of the followers was a young scientist, Jean-François Pilâtre de Rozier, who was convinced by the flight that it was now time for human beings to take over from the livestock.

De Rozier faced a problem – the king was still banning flights by humans. No one in France had ever experienced being at a high altitude. The country had mountains – Mont Blanc has its summit at 4,807m, but this was before the age of mountaineering and no one had ever stood there. The general belief was that the air consisted of a certain layer that undulated with the land – in other words, the air above Mont Blanc would be exactly the same density as that above the deepest valley. There was therefore a real possibility that a balloon starting at a low level would rise above the air layer since no one knew how far it reached.

The Montgolfiers were still keen on trying a manned flight, but first they had to convince the king. He was prepared to agree, provided that the flight would carry convicts who volunteered for the experiment with the promise of a complete pardon – that is, if they survived, which Louis clearly thought highly unlikely. When de Rozier heard of this plan he was incensed. He could not believe that the honour of being the first humans to fly should go to criminals.

De Rozier had an interesting career, one which would eventually take him into court circles, from an unlikely beginning. He was born at Metz in north-east France in 1754, where his farther, an ex-soldier, kept an inn. This was a garrison town, so he did well, and Jean-François became interested in the local army hospital, and in particular, the drugs being used. He decided to become a scientist, and his father was able to pay for him to go to Paris at the age of 18 to study chemistry and physics. He went on to teach the subjects at the Academy in Reims. While there he got to know the Comte de Provence, Louis XIV's brother, who gave him a post organising his Cabinet of Natural History. He continued his own studies, especially working on gases and had a favourite party trick: he would inhale hydrogen, blow it out and ignite it in a spectacular burst of flame. His connections with the aristocracy were now to prove crucial to his ambitions.

De Rozier managed to persuade the Duchess of Polignac to argue his case. She had arrived at court in 1775 and had quickly become a favourite companion of Marie Antoinette – an ideal person to gain the attention of the king. Another aristocratic advocate joined in, the Marquis d'Arlandes, an officer in the Royal Guard. He just made one stipulation – he would join de Rozier for the flight. Finally, the king agreed and the project could go ahead.

The news must have been greeted by the Montgolfiers with mixed feelings. Their dream of manned flight was about to be tested, but at the same time, the lives of two young men – both of whom had highly influential friends – depended on them. De Rozier was inevitably equally concerned and took a great personal interest in the construction of the balloon that would carry him aloft.

Not a great deal is known about the details, but it seems the fabric of the balloon was slightly heavier and stronger than on previous versions. The only figures quoted for size were in English units – 75ft high by 45ft diameter. The fire was contained in a wrought-iron basket, slung below the balloon, attached by chains, and surrounded by a wickerwork basket forming a gallery for the aeronauts from which they could feed the fire. The fuel favoured by the Montgolfiers was a mixture of wool and straw, providing adequate heat but with little risk of sparks creating a disaster. It had exotic decoration in blue and gold and was emblazoned with signs of the zodiac.

The balloon was again to be made at Faubourg St-Antoine in the French suburbs, near enough to the city centre for crowds to gather outside the factory in the hope of seeing what was going on. The *Journal de Paris* was rather scathing in its comments, suggesting that there was nothing much to see and even if hoi polloi did see something they would not be able to understand it. That did not stop the curious from turning up anyway.

On 15 October 1783, the fire was lit for the first time, the tethered balloon inflated and de Rozier climbed into the gallery. The balloon was allowed to lift a short distance, but de Rozier's weight on one side made it dangerously unstable. It was lowered and ballast added to the other side. It was now allowed to rise to a height of nearly 30m, the full extent of the tether, before being brought to settle gently back to earth. As soon as it hit the ground, the delighted de Rozier leapt out, leaving everything unstable. Without his weight, it shot up again, but fortunately the ropes held, and it did not disappear to distant horizons.

There was a second ascent the same day without mishaps. Now the crowd outside had been rewarded for their patience. They gathered again the next day, but with a strong breeze blowing, no attempts were made.

Over the next few days there were more tethered ascents, one of which produced a near accident. A sudden gust of wind blew the balloon into a nearby tree, but de Rozier simply added more straw to the fire and the balloon lifted clear of the branches.

On Sunday, 9 October, the ballast was removed and its place was taken by Giroud de Villette. After his flight, it was now the turn of the Marquis d'Arlandes to take his place in the basket to prepare for the real flight.

On 20 November, the balloon was taken to the grounds of the Château de la Muette, home of the dauphin in the Bois de Boulogne. It was supposed to be a very private affair, only to be watched by the dauphin and his invited friends, but inevitably news leaked out and crowds began to gather. The start was delayed by bad weather, and the Montgolfiers felt it necessary to have at least one more tethered flight at the new site as a precaution. Once again the weather proved fickle, and a breeze almost carried the balloon away. It was secured but damaged.

The Montgolfiers had allowed for such accidents and already had a small army of seamstresses on hand to make repairs. In two hours, everything was ready and by early afternoon, the wind had dropped, the sky had cleared and there were to be no further delays. The two men climbed aboard and at 2.54 p.m. they took off for the historic flight.

The balloon rose and was carried by a light wind towards the Seine and the two men waved enthusiastically to the crowds in the streets below them. They seemed entirely happy with this new experience, but things soon started to get worryingly wrong, as was made clear in an account of the flight by the marquis.

At first, he wrote, they were hardly aware of the movement until they looked back and discovered that Château de la Muette was out of sight and they were drifting gently over the confluence of the rivers Oise and Seine. The marquis admitted

Pilâtre de Rozier on the first manned flight in a balloon.

that he was so besotted with admiring this unique view of the city that he often forgot that he also had to help keep the fire burning or they might have a closer view of the Seine than they wanted.

The first alarming sign of things to come was a sudden loud, cracking noise, but that turned out to be nothing more than a gust. A second crack, however, was more ominous and it turned out that one of the supporting cords had snapped. Inspection of the balloon showed some small, smouldering holes where embers from the fire had hit the cloth. These were doused with sponges but more alarmingly, the balloon appeared to be parting company from its supporting circle. Closer inspection showed that only two cords were broken and enough remained to hold everything together.

The marquis felt that the safest thing would be to land immediately, but de Rozier knew that they absolutely needed to find a safe landing place and until one appeared they were better off up in the air. He spotted a likely spot in a gap between two mills and came down safely – the marquis jumped clear, but his companion ended up under the collapsed balloon. He crawled out to be greeted by the Duc de Chartres, who had followed their progress on horseback. They had landed in what is now the 13th Arrondissement in the south-east of Paris, 5km from their starting point. The great adventure was over – men had flown.

Inevitably, other flights soon followed, and in 1784, the first of several intrepid women took to the skies. A flight had been planned to be piloted by a Monsieur Fleurant and the Count de Laurencin, but that gentleman decided the whole thing was far too dangerous. Élisabeth Thimble, an opera singer, was invited to take his place. She agreed and arrived at the launch site dressed as Minerva, but instead of the goddess's helmet she sported an immense flowered hat. She proved to be the ideal partner in the venture, helping to stoke the fire and joining with Fleurant in a couple of duets from Monsigny's opera, *La Belle Arsène*. The landing proved awkward, and she suffered a sprained ankle, but won herself a place in aviation history.

The Montgolfiers gave exhibitions of their balloons in various places and began what was to be the lasting appeal of hot-air ballooning. The modern balloon is not so very different from those of the brothers: the material for the envelope has changed and the heat is supplied by a gas burner rather than an open fire, but the principle remains the same.

The Montgolfiers had attempted to design a balloon with a complex shape for their first flight, but abandoned that in favour of the conventional, roughly spherical shape that is still in use today. But balloon design has developed in ways that would astonish the Montgolfiers. A whole variety of exotic shapes can now be produced and as a regular visitor to the Bristol Balloon Festival, I have seen some remarkable examples, from a gigantic Rupert Bear to a flying motor car, and was once treated to the appropriate sight of a six-pack of lager being pursued by Alka-Seltzers.

Ballooning is probably more popular today than it has ever been, but it still suffers from one problem – the balloon cannot be steered. It will only go where the wind takes it, which can create some interesting problems, as I discovered on my first flight. The pilot and I set off from a field near the Thames at Goring and floated along merrily until the pilot announced that we needed to land as soon as a safe site could be spotted. There was no problem with the balloon, but our track was going to take us right over the missile silos at the US air base at Greenham Common, where there was every chance we would receive a less than welcome reception.

If the problem of steering a hot-air balloon is unsolvable, that is not true of its rival, which went into development immediately after the Montgolfiers' first flight. News of it soon reached Paris and was met with considerable scepticism as scientific opinion did not believe that hot air alone could achieve such a result. We know that gases, including air, are composed of molecules, and when heat is applied, they speed up, either expanding their container or bursting it. That a balloon had gone up was certainly true – too many people had seen it for it not to be so – but the news encouraged others to try a different method, this time with a hydrogen balloon.

Jacques Charles was the first to try, helped by his two brothers, Ainé and Cadet. He proposed using a fabric coated with rubber solution. He then had to make the hydrogen, using iron filings treated with sulphuric acid. His balloon was much smaller than the Montgolfiers' – just 4m in diameter, it still required almost 500lb of acid and 1,000lb of iron to create enough gas.

Making the gas was one thing but getting it into the balloon proved the biggest problem. The first attempt involved mixing the materials in lead-lined boxes, connected to the balloon by a series of pipes. Unfortunately, more gas leaked from the pipes than arrived at the balloon. It was then decided to use a single pipe connecting the reaction boxes to a collecting barrel and from there by another pipe to the balloon. But adding the acid to the metal was an exothermic reaction, one which generated a great deal of heat, and to stop the balloon fabric catching fire it had to be regularly doused with water, some of which turned into steam that crept into the balloon and condensed. At the end of a whole day's activity, the balloon was still not ready to fly.

The next day was again spent filling the balloon and it was only the day after that that the balloon was given a trial tethered flight. Charles had calculated that the balloon could lift a weight of 35lb but it only managed a modest 21lb and by the end of the day, that had reduced to 18lb. It appeared some of the acid fumes had been carried over with the hydrogen and weakened the fabric.

Eventually, the balloon was allowed to rise, held by a rope, and it reached a height of over 30m. The Montgolfiers had not yet demonstrated their balloon in the capital, so the sight of a giant balloon bobbing up above the rooftops of Paris caused immense excitement and crowds gathered round Charles's yard, although they were kept safely outside.

The following day, the balloon was taken with a mounted escort in a torchlit procession to the Champ de Mars, an area best known today as the site of the Eiffel Tower. Once again, there were delays as the balloon was again topped up with hydrogen and the actual flight was scheduled for the following day, 28 August. Once it was released the balloon rose rapidly to a height of 1,000m and drifted off to eventually land 16.5km away at the village of Gonesse. Unfortunately, the locals decided that it was a monster come to attack them and completely destroyed the invader.

Jacques Charles was convinced that the hydrogen balloon was superior to the hot-air version. It had travelled further than the Montgolfier, but it had taken days to prepare, while the rival had been made ready for flight in less than an hour. To prove his point, he now needed to make a manned flight. He was to be joined by Nicolas-Louis Robert, and they planned to leave from the Jardin des Tuileries on 1 December 1783, where one of the ornamental lakes in the gardens had been covered over as a launching platform.

He had made a number of changes since the first flight. The next spherical balloon was made of rubberised silk and its resemblance to a globe gave the names south and north pole to bottom and top. A valve at the south pole allowed gas to escape as the balloon rose to higher altitudes where the air was

Charles and Robert leaving the Jardin de Tuileries in their hydrogen balloon. (Library of Congress)

thinner, and one at the north pole connected by a rope to the gondola could be opened to allow a gentle descent.

The two men had no idea what to expect when they set off so they took provisions, including a great deal of wine, heavy clothing and blankets to keep warm, a thermometer and a barometer to measure the height. The balloon, not surprisingly, rose much more rapidly than the Montgolfier, reaching a height of around 1,000ft, where they discovered the temperature was a comfortable 12°C, so they jettisoned the blankets, one of which ended up draped over the dome of a church.

As they soared above Paris, they waved flags to the watching crowds and shouted, 'Long live the king!'. Eventually, they left Paris behind and decided to make a descent onto what appeared to be an empty plain. The north pole valve was opened, and everything was going well until they realised there was a solitary tree directly in their path. Charles simply threw out one of the ballast bags, and the balloon rose above the branches and was then settled comfortably down on the ground on the far side. It was a success, but Jacques Charles never flew again.

Following these early successes, many more came forward to make flights, among whom was the flamboyant Vincenzo Lunardi, who arrived in England as part of the entourage of the Neapolitan Ambassador. He made several flights in different parts of Britain, and he was the first to try to come up with a method of steering the balloon. He added oars to the gondola, but this was never going to succeed. He also attained a certain notoriety when he set off in the company of a young actress, Letitia Anne Sage. During the flight, they picnicked and consumed several bottles of wine, which were simply thrown overboard. The event caused a great deal of scurrilous gossip on what else they might have been up to out of sight in the sky. There was, it has to be said, no evidence that they were pioneering members of the Mile-High Club.

Another early pioneer was Pierre Blanchard, whose first attempt at flying consisted of building what he called a 'velocipede' when he was just 16 years old. This was a four-wheeled vehicle fitted with two pairs of flapping wings, one pair worked by a foot treadle, the other by hand levers. He claimed that it took off and skimmed above the ground – but no one witnessed this unlikely event. When he heard of the successful balloon flights, he decided to build a balloon of his own and fit that with wings, which would enable him to steer it wherever he chose.

At his first attempt, he declared that he would take off from Paris and steer a course that would land him at La Villette, to the north of the capital. The wings were no match for the wind that took him a short distance in the opposite direction before his flight came to an end. He was determined, however, to prove himself the world's greatest aviator and moved to England, where he planned to make the first crossing of the Channel.

He and a companion, Thomas Sadler, left Dover on 7 January 1785 in a hydrogen balloon equipped with the usual wings. The flight was slow and to maintain height they were constantly having to throw out ballast. When all that had gone, they jettisoned whatever they could, from the useless wings to their heavy greatcoats. Fortunately, the weather changed, the balloon rose, and they achieved their goal of being the first to fly across the Channel.

Blanchard tried to cash in on his fame by staging exhibition flights but with no great success. He tried to gather bigger crowds by including his wife Sophie in the performances. When her husband died in 1809, she continued on her own, using a small balloon and standing in a minute

Sophie Blanchard dressed in style, rising in the tiny gondola beneath the balloon. Tragically, she died when giving a display with fireworks from the balloon. (Library of Congress)

gondola. She became famous but in July 1819 she planned a spectacular flight from the Tivoli Gardens in Paris. As she rose, she would unfurl a flag and begin a firework display using 'Bengal fire'. Fireworks and a highly flammable gas are not a good combination. The balloon caught fire. She might have survived, as the descent was slow, but the balloon caught on a rooftop and tipped her off her tiny perch and she fell to her death.

Over the years, there were several attempts to turn hydrogen balloons into steerable airships, but success depended on finding a suitable power source that was also light enough to be practical. The answer was eventually found with the internal combustion engine. The most important developer was unquestionably Ferdinand Graf von Zeppelin, who was born in 1838. After a successful army career which ended with his being appointed to the command of a cavalry regiment, he resigned and began designing airships, which were given the designation LZ, followed by their number.

After two unsuccessful attempts, in 1907 LZ3, powered by two 85hp engines, stayed aloft for eight hours, travelling at an average speed of around 30mph. There were to be further improvements over the next few years.

Then, in 1914, the Zeppelin took on a new and more sinister role. Joseph Montgolfier had contemplated using balloons to carry troops to capture a garrison. The Zeppelins, however, carried bombs not troops, which they dropped on targets in Britain in the First World War.

After the end of the war, airships began to be developed to carry passengers on long-distance flights, including transatlantic crossings between Europe and the United States. One of the appeals of the service was that passengers could enjoy the sort of luxury they had once enjoyed on ocean liners – minus the seasickness.

The days of the airships were short-lived, however. The loss of both the British R 101 and the Zeppelin *Hindenburg*, which both ended in an inferno of burning hydrogen, effectively brought it to an end. In future, inflammable hydrogen would have to be replaced by the next lightest element – the inert gas helium. This, in effect, meant that to carry the same load as a hydrogen airship, it would have to be twice as big, and this was no longer financially viable.

A modern Zeppelin coming in to land at the Zeppelin Museum at Friedrichshafen. (Author)

Airships are still manufactured and do still fly. Some years ago, I visited the Zeppelin Museum at Friedrichshafen, close to the site of the original Zeppelin factory. The first thing I saw when I arrived was a small Zeppelin lifting off with a tourist flight over Lake Constance.

Lighter-than-air flying machines have come a long way since the Montgolfiers sent up their first balloon. Jacques-Étienne died in 1799, and the business passed to his son-in-law, Barthélémy de Canson. He established a new mill at Annonay, which still exists, specialising in high-quality art paper. Joseph-Michel died in 1810. The brothers have a place of honour at the International Space Hall of Fame in San Diego, California.

4

THE MARQUIS DE JOUFFROY D'ABBANS

The designer of the first paddle steamer, the first vessel of any kind to be powered by steam.

This French nobleman had a suitably imposing name – Claude-François-Dorothée, Marquis de Jouffroy d'Abbans. He was born in the Champagne region of France but was brought up near Besançon, where his aristocratic family owned the castle. The area was noted for clock and watch-making and it is said that while he was there he took the clock from the castle tower to pieces and reassembled it.

Despite his interest in all things mechanical, a career in engineering was not seen as appropriate for a boy of his status. The family decided that the army was the place for him and at the age of 13 he was sent off to the Palace of Versailles to act as a page and receive military instruction. As it turned out, this was a fortunate move, because among his instructors was the mathematician Louis Trincano, author of the standard work on useful mathematics for the army – a manual intended to show the use of mathematics in the practical world, which was invaluable information for a would-be engineer.

On completing his time at Versailles, d'Abbans was given a commission in an infantry regiment. Things did not turn out well. He and his commanding officer, it seems, had eyes on the same lady and the rivalry ended in some form of altercation – some accounts say a duel, others suggest a brawl. Whichever the case, the army was not going to let a second lieutenant fight a superior officer. He was court-martialled and sent to prison in the Forte Sainte-Marguerite, off the coast near Cannes. He was there for two years and, in popular accounts, it was here that he spent his time looking out and seeing galleys rowed by teams of sweating men and began to think whether there might be a better way to move a vessel through the water. He also had time to study subjects such as navigation, which he felt might be useful when he was released and left the army.

In 1773, he was released from prison and made his way to Paris, where he made the acquaintance of the Périer brothers, who had formed the idea of a water company that would use steam power to pump water to the citizens of Paris. Here we must take a detour to Britain to see how the idea of steam power was first developed.

The coal and mineral mines of Britain were having to go ever deeper but as they did so, they were faced with ever greater volumes of water to be pumped out before the extraction could start. For centuries, the mines had depended on pump rods, worked via waterwheels, but these were no longer adequate.

The first successful alternative was devised by Thomas Newcomen of Dartmouth in Devon, who had a thriving ironmonger business, mainly supplying tools for the local mines, so he was well aware of the problem. His solution was

The Marquis de Jouffroy d'Abbans by an unknown artist. (CCA SA 3.0 via Wikimedia Commons)

a basic form of steam engine. The pumping action for the mines depended on pump rods moving up and down. Gravity took care of the downward part of the movement but some form of force was needed to lift the rods, before releasing them to drop again.

His engine consisted of a huge overhead beam, pivoting on a central support. The pump rods were hung from one end and a piston, sitting snugly in an open-topped cylinder was suspended from the other. Steam was forced into the cylinder below the piston, then doused with cold water. The steam condensed, creating a partial vacuum, and air pressure pushed the piston down, the beam rocked, and the pump rods rose. Once the pressure equalised, the rods fell again and the whole cycle could be repeated.

The first of these nodding giants was installed at the Earl of Dudley's colliery at Dudley in the Black Country in 1712. Soon these engines were to be found at work at mines throughout the country.

The Newcomen engine could more accurately be called an atmospheric engine rather than a true steam engine, as the actual force was provided by air pressure. It did the job it was invented for but suffered from one disadvantage – it was remarkably inefficient. This was not a problem at coal mines, where fuel was readily available, but was more of a headache for the mineral mines of Devon and Cornwall.

This type of engine was the first that d'Abbans saw and he began to devise a means of using it to power a boat. The problem with the Newcomen engine was that it was not very well adapted to anything more than pumping, so to produce rotary motion, a falling weight would have to be used to replace the pump rods and then they would need to be transferred to create rotary action. One method could have been to attach a ratchet to the falling weight to engage with a cog, and this seems to be what d'Abbans did on his first experimental boat.

His next decision was how to move his craft through the water. It was said that during his exile in Provence he had watched convicts rowing galleys, which was the inspiration for thinking of an alternative way of moving a craft. It has to be said that this may simply be another piece of folklore, but he certainly became interested in the idea of mechanical oars.

He also looked to the natural world for inspiration, much as the first would-be aviators had tried to fly using feathered wings. He planned to imitate the action of waterfowl, by equipping his boat with weblike paddles. He even named it the *Palmipède* – the Webfoot. The vessel was 13m long, and the powered oars had hinged flaps to create the paddling effect. It was tested on the River Doubs in eastern France during June and July 1776, between Besançon and Montbéliard. Not surprisingly, it failed to live up to expectations, being notably sluggish. There were two problems: one was the choice of oars for propulsion; the other was the inefficiency of the Newcomen engine. It had a fundamental flaw that made it unsuitable for the job.

There had been various attempts to improve the Newcomen engine, but none of them attacked the root of the problem. This was left to James Watt, so we must return to Britain for the next stage of the story.

One can forget the popular stories of young James seeing steam lifting the lid of a pot in his mother's kitchen and being inspired to invent the steam engine. The truth is less fanciful, but more satisfactory. He was presented with a problem and used his brain to come up with a solution and then doggedly pursued his idea to produce an engine that changed the world.

Watt had trained as a maker of scientific instruments and was appointed Mechanical Instrument Maker at the University of

Glasgow. It was in this role in the academic year 1763–64 that he was sent a model of a Newcomen engine that obstinately refused to work. He recognised that the problem was fundamental: a lot of the energy that should be employed making the machine work was being wasted in constantly having to reheat the cylinder after each stroke of the piston. The answer came to him, he later recorded, when he was strolling around Glasgow Green. Here is his own description of the event in *Aris's Birmingham Gazette*, February 1796: 'The idea came into my mind that as steam is an elastic body it would rush into a vacuum, and if a communication was made between the cylinder and an exhausted vessel it would rush into it and would there be condensed without cooling the cylinder.'

The separate condenser was key to the success of his proposal, but there remained the problem of heat loss from the open-topped cylinder. If he closed that off, then air pressure would not act on the piston. He could, however, use steam pressure instead. The atmospheric engine could become a true steam engine.

Many inventors fail to profit from their ideas, but Watt was fortunate in finding the ideal business partner in Matthew Boulton. Boulton had a factory in Birmingham, manufacturing 'toys', not playthings but small decorative metal items, such as buckles and buttons. Initially, Watt had suggested they might get together to make steam engines for the English Midlands but Boulton had far greater ambitions, as he explained in a letter to Watt on 7 July 1796: 'It would not be worth my while to make for three counties only, but I find it well worth my while to make for all the world.' And that is what they did from a new factory built beside the Birmingham Canal at Soho.

The success of the new engines attracted the attention of Jacques-Constantin Périer, who had formed a company to

A typical example of an eighteenth-century Boulton & Watt steam engine used for pumping water from mines.

supply water from the Seine, which would be pumped by steam engine to customers in Paris. The normal method of supply used by Boulton & Watt was to send essential parts of the engine and leave it to the customer to construct by following an instruction book. The parts were shipped in 1781 and soon water was flowing to the paying customers and supplying seven public fountains in the city. And now we can return to the Périer brothers' friend, the Marquis de Jouffroy d'Abbans.

He now had an appropriate engine, and he must have real-ised that his web-footed oars had not been a success. There was an alternative device that involved water and power that had been in use for centuries. Water pushed the wheel round and provided power for machinery. If he reversed the process and used machinery to turn a wheel in water, then the water would be forced away from the boat – and simple Newtonian physics tells us that every action has an equal and opposite reaction, so the boat would move forward.

He built a paddle steamer, which was called *Pyroscaphe* – Fireboat. Although later models were made, little is really known about the actual specifications of the craft, although there is a model made by the inventor and some drawings survive. It is generally agreed that it was 13m long and 4.5m

A model of the paddle steamer *Pyroscaphe* in the Musée de la Marine de Paris. (Arnaud 25, CCA SA 4.0 via Wikimedia Commons)

beam. We do know that the single-cylinder steam engine was similar to the Boulton & Watt in some ways, but it was placed horizontally rather than vertically, and instead of relying on an overhead beam, it was attached by a piston rod to a ratchet system to turn a shaft to which to the two paddle wheels were attached.

The first trial run took place on the River Saône at Lyon on 16 July 1783. At first, the boat performed well, achieving a respectable speed estimated at around 6 knots. However, problems soon appeared, with leaks in the hull and escaping steam. The boat was steered ashore and repairs made and soon d'Abbans was able to make more successful runs with invited passengers. The latter signed documents to confirm that they had indeed travelled under steam power alone.

The inventor had hoped to get official recognition for his invention from the French Academy of Sciences, but the dignitaries declined to visit Lyon and refused permission for him to demonstrate the boat on the Seine in Paris. To justify his claim, he sent a model to the academy, which is now in the National Maritime Museum in Paris, together with the signed statements from the passengers. He was not successful.

He might have been able to continue developing his ideas, but France was about to be plunged into revolution. It was not a time for suggesting developing steamboats – and certainly not a time for an aristocrat to step forward. His hopes of obtaining a patent from the revolutionary government were nil, and as an ardent royalist, he refused to apply to the new ruler, Napoleon, who he regarded as a treacherous usurper. He ended his days in a home for army veterans, the Hotel des Invalides in Paris, where he died in 1832.

Although d'Abbans failed to capitalise on his invention, it spurred others to emulate his success. In Britain, William Symington built a small paddle steamer, which was given a trial on a lake near Dumfries in 1788. Among the passengers was the poet Robert Burns who, alas, failed to celebrate the occasion in verse. The experiment had been promoted by Patrick Miller of Dalswinton, but he was reluctant to take the idea into any further development.

News of the idea came to the attention of Lord Dundas, Governor of the Forth & Clyde Canal Company. He suggested that Symington should build an engine for installation in a boat of a type designed by Captain John Schank of the Royal Navy, which had a sliding keel, making it usable both at sea and in shallow water. The idea would be to use it as a tugboat on the canal. The boat had a vertical cylinder, transmitting the drive through crossheads to the paddle wheels.

Trials on the River Carron in 1801 were partly successful, but there were problems, and a second boat was built to a different design and named *Charlotte Dundas*. The main difference was that it now had an engine with a horizontal 22in cylinder, driving a crank to a single central enclosed wheel in the hull.

In March 1802, the steam tug hauled a pair of 70-ton barges along the canal against a strong headwind, covering 20 miles on the canal in around six hours. It was a respectable effort, but the authorities were ultimately unimpressed and felt the advantages were outweighed by the danger of the churned-up water eroding the canal banks. Twenty years after d'Abbans' pioneering work, no steamer had yet gone into commercial service. However, that was about to change.

Robert Fulton was born in Pennsylvania in 1765, while the United States was still a British colony. He showed early signs of developing an interest in engineering but earned his living as a painter of portraits and landscapes. In 1786, bad health, thought to have been incipient tuberculosis, saw him moving to France. He continued painting, but also began working on

The steam paddle tug *Charlotte Dundas*, which was given trials on the Forth
& Clyde Canal. (Drawn by John Cook Bourne; B. Woodcroft, 'Steam
Navigation' in *Transactions of the Society for the Encouragement of Arts &c.*,
Vol. 1(1846–1847). (CCA SA 4.0 via Wikimedia Commons)

various practical problems, including an attempt to design
a submarine.

Britain was now at the height of the Industrial Revolution
and the 1790s became known as the years of canal mania,
with new waterways being built around the country. He met
the Duke of Bridgewater, who was interested in developing
steam vessels for use on his canal – but the experiments proved
unsatisfactory and the duke eventually ordered vessels similar
to *Charlotte Dundas*.

In the United States, the idea of steamships was also being
discussed, and Robert Livingston, a member of the five-man

committee that drafted the Declaration of Independence, obtained exclusive rights to operate steamboats on the Hudson River – though he had no such vessels at the time. He contacted Fulton, who built a small steamer that was given trials on the Seine. Fulton always acknowledged that he was following in the watery footsteps of d'Abbans.

Back in the United States, work began on building a larger passenger vessel, *Clermont*, and we have Fulton's own description of the specifications, 'My first steamboat on the Hudson's River was 150 feet long, 13 feet wide drawing 2ft of water, bow and stern 60 degrees she displaced 36–40 cubic feet equal to 100 tons of water' (quoted in Alice Sutcliffe, *Robert Fulton and the Clermont*, 1909). There were three cabins with fifty-four berths and a kitchen for serving meals on board. The vertical engine was provided by Boulton & Watt and drove two side paddles.

The first voyage set off from New York on 17 August 1807 for a round trip of 300 miles to Albany and back, travelling at an average speed of 5mph. It went into regular service the following month.

The success of Fulton's vessel marked the start of regular steamboat services on other rivers, notably the Mississippi, with its famous stern-wheelers – a steam-powered paddle vessel, *Natchez*, still operates out of New Orleans.

Fulton's venture encouraged Henry Bell, who owned a hotel at Helensburgh, to contemplate running a similar service to take citizens of Glasgow away from the city to enjoy healthy sea air – including visiting his hotel. He was already friendly with David Napier, who had a foundry at Dumbarton and agreed to manufacture an engine and boiler. The vessel went into service between Glasgow and Helensburgh in 1812. It ran ashore off Craignish Point when returning from a trip to Fort William to the great delight of a local minister, who

A 1909 replica of *Clermont*, the first successful commercial paddle steamer in the United States. (Detroit Publishing Company photograph collection, Library of Congress)

wrote of Bell (detailed in an undated newspaper cutting in the Glasgow Museum of Transport Archives):

> He being puffed up in pride of his abilities, did lately conceive a ship to go upon the waters, nit be dint of the clean winds of the air as ordained by God, but by means of fire and a great smoke which issues from the bowels thereof.

Comet was to be first of a long line of steamers that would take Glaswegians 'doon th' water'. The last of these, *Waverley*, is also the last seagoing paddle steamer in the world. It would certainly have amazed and possibly delighted d'Abbans

– where his pioneering vessel could just about squeeze half a dozen passengers on board, *Waverley* can carry over 900. The former's simple single-cylinder engine would be dwarfed by the mighty triple-expansion 2,100hp engine. His basic idea of a steam engine being used to turn paddle wheels has not changed in its fundamentals in over 200 years.

Waverley, the last seagoing paddle steamer in the world, seen here off the English coast. (Robert Mason)

5

RICHARD TREVITHICK

*The Cornish engineer who built the first
steam locomotive to run on rails.*

Richard Trevithick was born at Illogan in Cornwall in April 1771, in an area dominated by tin and copper mines. The family moved to Penponds, on the outskirts of Camborne, shortly after his birth. His father, also Richard, was a mine captain, in effect, the engineer in charge of all the mine machinery. He was well acquainted with the Newcomen engines that were in use throughout the region for draining mines and felt quite free to improve on the original design with alterations of his own – this was a confidence in his own abilities that he would pass on to his son.

Young Richard was, it seems, a precocious boy, quick to learn in subjects that interested him, such as mathematics, but less interested in other subjects – his spelling remained erratic throughout his life. The limited resources of the local school meant that he was far more interested in learning the practical details of mining than he was in book work. He left school as soon as he could and his name appears in the wage book of Dalcoath Mine when he was just 15 years old.

Richard rose rapidly in the mining world, helped no doubt by family influence, but reinforced by his own undoubted abilities. He grew up tall and strong – his party piece was an ability to throw a sledgehammer over an engine-house roof. It was a time of turmoil in Cornwall – the discovery of huge quantities of high-grade copper ore at Parys Mountain on Anglesey affected the Cornish industry, and everyone was looking for ways to cut costs.

The Newcomen engine had largely been replaced by the more efficient Boulton & Watt and the company charged for its use. There were engineers who felt they could produce better, more efficient engines, one of whom, Jonathan Hornblower, built an engine of his own. However, he fell foul of Watt's all-embracing patent and was forced to abandon his experiment.

Young Trevithick was one of those who was impressed by the Hornblower engine and was tempted to find ways of building better engines himself. In 1791, another engineer, Edward Bull, arrived from a colliery in Coventry to erect a Boulton & Watt engine. He remained in the county and began experimenting with a new type of engine, finding an enthusiastic ally in Trevithick.

Instead of the massive overhead beam, the steam cylinder was inverted over the shaft, with a simple connecting rod from the piston to the pit work that activated the pump. It certainly looked quite unlike a Boulton & Watt engine, but there was no getting away from the fact that it used a separate condenser, which was specifically covered by the Watt patent.

At first, Watt was quite unconcerned, but when Trevithick and Bull began claiming that their engine was far superior, the law was invoked. Bull received a writ and was legally banned

Richard Trevithick.

from installing his engine, or any other, but it made no mention of Trevithick. He started work installing an engine at Ding Dong Mine, an isolated site, high on the moors near Land's End. There is a story that attempts were made to serve a writ on Trevithick, but it appears that the unfortunate emissary who had orders to either present it in person or pin it on the engine-house door was spotted long before he got to the lonely mine. He was picked up and dangled by his feet over the shaft, at which point he wisely decided not to carry out his duty.

Trevithick had many qualities, but caution was not one of them. He decided to visit Birmingham to see what was going on there but he was recognised and the writ was served. That particular project was at an end.

It did not mean, however, that he had abandoned the idea of building a better engine than Watt's and setting it to work. He had worked on a new type of pump before again returning to thinking about improving the steam engine. What, he wondered, would be the result of removing the separate condenser altogether and simply relying on steam power alone? He asked a friend, Davies Gilbert, what power would be lost if he used steam at several atmospheric pressures and simply allowed the exhaust steam to escape – to which Davies replied that it would be just one atmosphere. Davies recalled that when he gave his opinion, 'he never saw a man more delighted'.

Trevithick set about building his first high-pressure engine, starting with a model that was put through its trials on the kitchen table at his home. A local mine owner, who had recently been created a peer, Lord de Dunstanville, took an interest in the experiment. The honour of stoking the fire went to Davies and opening the valve to let the steam into the model went to Lady de Dunstanville.

It was a success, and the first full-scale version was constructed and set to work at Ding Dong. The portable engines were known as 'puffers' because of the way the steam was simply blown out into the air. Where a Boulton & Watt engine was supplying steam at around 3psi, Trevithick's was working at 50psi, so it required a new type of boiler to withstand the pressure inside which a tube was set, taking hot gases from the firebox. It was bent into a U-shape and the exhaust passed up a chimney at the firebox end. As a result of the use of high-pressure steam, the engines were much smaller than the older type of engine.

Trevithick's next step appears to have been inspired by the sight of one of his engines being wheeled away to its site. It made him think that perhaps the engine could be adapted to move itself. Up to then, vehicles had moved either by being pulled or pushed. He knew his engine could be used to turn a wheel, but would a turning wheel simply go round or would there be enough friction to also move the vehicle. He made a simple experiment – he turned a cartwheel by hand, and the cart moved. He now had all the information he needed to build a steam road locomotive.

He was not actually the first to produce such a machine. A former officer of the Austro-Hungarian Empire, Nicolas Cugnot, had the idea of building a steam tractor to haul guns. His prototype was built in 1769, and an improved version appeared a year later. It is a cumbersome device, mounted on three wheels with the drive applied to the single front wheel and a copper boiler suspended over it, supplying steam to cylinders on either side of the wheel. It was not a success and was never adopted, though the second engine has pride of place in the Musée des Arts et Métiers in Paris. News of the invention does not seem to have reached Britain, and even if it had, the Trevithick machine had very little in common with the French invention.

The tabletop model of Trevithick's 'puffer' portable steam engine.
(The Steam Museum, Straffan, Ireland)

Trevithick set to work building a full-sized road locomotive. The steam cylinder was cast at Harvey's in Hayle. A local blacksmith, Jonathan Tyack was employed and some of the work was done by his friend Andrew Vivian in his personal workshop. No drawings or illustrations have survived, but the surviving model was almost certainly the basis for the working engine. The cylinder was set in the middle of the return-flue boiler, as in the puffers and steam controlled through a four-way cock. A crosshead above the piston was attached to connecting rods taking the drive to the wheels. The engine was steered by means of a tiller. A full-sized working replica was built to mark the bicentenary, and on that, a system of pegs was used, against which the tiller could rest to hold it in place when rounding corners – not an easy task, as was to be proved dramatically later with the original.

The great day of the trial was Christmas Eve 1801, and a first-hand account tells of six or seven people jumping on the engine as it puffed its way up Camborne hill for half a mile before turning round and coming back again. The eyewitness reported that 'she was going faster than I could walk'. The day was a triumph, but a short-lived one. (Incidentally, the event is celebrated in the popular Cornish song, 'Going Up Camborne Hill Going Down'.)

On Boxing Day, Trevithick and Vivian set off for the de Dunstanville home at Tehidy, 2 miles from Camborne, to show off the invention to the family there. They were about halfway there when the engine ran into a watercourse crossing the road. The tiller was jerked out of Vivian's hand and the engine overturned. It happened near an inn, where the two men went to have a drink and decide what to do next. Unfortunately, they had neglected to put out the fire – the boiler exploded, and the engine was destroyed. Luckily, it was not quite the tragedy it might have been, for this had

Replica of the original road locomotive manned by members of the Trevithick Society. (Trevithick Society)

always been a prototype made simply to test the idea of a steam carriage.

Trevithick now set out on his real project – a steam coach that would be the world's first horseless carriage. The new engine would be different in many ways from the Camborne. This time the cylinder was horizontal, and the piston rod was forked to allow for movement of the crankshaft that turned the rear wheels of the carriage. These were huge compared with those of other coaches of the day, at around 8ft, but this was needed to allow enough space to fit the engine beneath the chassis. Tiller steering was used again, but this time to a single small front wheel. The engine parts were all manufactured in Cornwall, but the coachwork was made by William Felton of Leather Lane in Clerkenwell, London.

The carriage needed a two-man crew – a steerer at the front and a stoker and driver at the rear. There was a demonstration run in Oxford Street, which was said to attract huge crowds, but not, alas, any potential investors.

There were still steering problems – on one trip, the carriage was going down Tottenham Court Road when it became out of control and removed several yards of iron railings from a garden wall. A sea captain who took a ride on it claimed that he felt far sicker in the carriage than he ever had on board ship. Was the ride really that bad or was it a result of the poorly paved streets?

As with the first engine, a replica has been made. It was brought up to London and Leather Lane for the unveiling of a plaque to mark the site of the Felton carriage works, and I was fortunate to join Frank Trevithick Okuno, a direct descendant of the great engineer, for a trip round Regent's Park. It was really very smooth and comfortable and rather grand as people stopped and stared at the strange apparition.

However, the original carriage came to nothing and it seemed there was no one interested in putting up the money – and no shortage of objectors to having newfangled noisy, smoky vehicles on the streets of the capital. Trevithick made no further attempts to develop road carriages.

The next stage of development for vehicles moved by steam is uncertain. It is known that Trevithick was in touch with the famous Darby Ironworks of Coalbrookdale about supplying them with a steam engine, which was to work at what was, for then, the remarkably high pressure of 145psi. At the same time, in a letter describing the engine written in August 1802, he added this comment (the spelling is the original), 'The Dale Co have begun a garage at their own cost for the real-roads' – presumably, the existing horse-drawn route from the works to the River Severn.

Model built by Tom Brogden of the London steam carriage. (Tom Brogden)

That is all we know for sure of the Coalbrookdale engine, although a drawing dated 1803 shows an engine with a 4¾in cylinder with a 3ft stroke, which fits very well a description written by a visitor to Coalbrookdale in 1884, who gave details of a 'cherished relic' of the locomotive that fits perfectly with the drawing. On that basis, a working replica of the engine was built and is run at the Blists Hill Museum. As with the London carriage, the cylinder is horizontal and the piston is connected to a crosshead, reaching across the engine, with connecting rods working through gears to the wheels on one side. The motion means that the working connecting rods go to and fro, like the slides of an oversized trombone, next to the driving position. I also had the privilege of being offered a ride on this engine and it is certainly a novel experience having those moving parts oscillating right next to the footplate. There are, however, no records of how it performed, but it seems certain that, successful or not, it was the world's first railway locomotive.

The next locomotive, however, is fully documented. The story begins with rivalry between two ironworks in south Wales: Samuel Homfray's Penydarren works and Richard Crawshay's Cyfarthfa works at Merthyr Tydfil. Both used the Glamorganshire Canal as the link to Cardiff, and there were constant arguments over who had the right of way when using the locks.

Homfray decided to solve the problem by building a tramway from the works, bypassing the troublesome locks to join the canal at Abercynon, 9½ miles away. Like other tramways at the time, the rails were of cast iron and mounted on rows of stone blocks, leaving a clear space in between for the horses that would do the work. As it was never intended to be part of any larger system, a gauge of 4ft 4in was chosen, which would be suitable for existing wagons.

Replica of the Coalbrookdale engine in steam at the Blists Hill
Victorian Town.

It was for this line that it was proposed to Trevithick that
he should build an engine, but it was to be more than just a
locomotive. When not in use on the tracks, it would be used
as a stationary engine in the works. Crawshay mocked the
whole idea and laid a bet with Homfray that it would not
work for the huge amount of 500 guineas, equivalent of over
£60,000 at today's prices. To win the wager, the locomotive
would have to take 10 tons of iron to Abercynon and return
with the empties.

Trevithick was confident of success and work began on
constructing the engine. In many ways, it was very similar to
the Coalbrookdale engine, but with a bigger engine – 8¾in
cylinder and 54in stroke – and a large flywheel that would
have been essential for use at the works. Unlike the puffers,
the exhaust steam was taken through a pipe to the bottom
of the chimney, which increased the airflow over the coals
in the firebox.

Trevithick sent full accounts of the trial back to Cornwall and on 8 February 1804, he was able to report that Crawshay had travelled with the engine and it had successfully brought the required 10 tons to Abercynon and returned to Merthyr. It was a triumph, although not a complete success. The problem was not with the engine but with the cast-iron rails, which tended to crack under the weight of the locomotive.

Nevertheless, news of the experiment travelled through the industrial world and another engine was ordered by Christopher Blackett of Wylam Colliery in Northumberland. However, once again, the problem was an engine that was too heavy for the rails and it never went into operation.

Trevithick's nature was always one of optimism; he was convinced his schemes would work. If the industrialists had a problem with it, perhaps the investors of London would finance his plans instead. He built a new engine – one that would never be required to work in a factory or foundry. This time, the single cylinder was set vertically in the boiler, and connecting rods took the drive directly to the rear wheels.

To demonstrate the new machine, he obtained the use of a plot of land near what would later be Euston Station, where he laid a circular track – and as horses were not involved, he was able to use wooden sleepers instead of stone blocks. The site was enclosed, and visitors were offered rides at a shilling a time. The locomotive was given the crowd-pleasing name *Catch-me-who-can* and tickets bore the message, 'Mechanical Power Subduing Animal Speed'.

But the temporary track proved as fallible as the permanent tracks of earlier trials and the whole experiment had to be abandoned, with no investors showing an interest. Trevithick was by now thoroughly disillusioned and gave up all attempts to develop his ideas any further – though he did acquire a patent for the locomotive.

Engraving of Trevithick's locomotive *Catch-me-who-can* giving rides to visitors at a site near the present Euston Station, London. (Cannasue via iStock)

The next part of life saw him engaged in a variety of different projects. In London, he was employed in several. He was engaged as chief engineer for a road tunnel under the Thames, for which he felt his mining experience would make it a simple task. However, in January 1809, there was a roof collapse, and the works were flooded. Typically, Trevithick remained underground among the rising waters until everyone else was safely out, after which he waded through the water to emerge covered in mud and minus his boots. Although he offered a solution for restarting the works, the company abandoned the project.

Other projects he worked on included a new type of dredger and an ingenious device for salvaging sunken vessels. A box full of water would be lowered and attached to the wreck and the air pumped out, at which point the box would rise, bringing the vessel with it. The system was given a successful trial at Margate, where a ship was successfully raised. Trevithick asked for his fee, but the ship's owners insisted that it had all been too easy, and he had to tow it back to harbour as well or he would get nothing. Disgusted, Trevithick ordered the crew to cut the lines, and the ship sank back to the bottom.

As so often in his life, Trevithick was full of new ideas but lacked the finance to carry them out – and in 1810, he suffered a life-threatening illness, described at the time as 'typhus and gastric fever'. He recovered but found that his financial affairs were in a catastrophic state. London had proved to be a long series of disappointments – it was time to return to Cornwall.

Back on home ground, his fortunes began to improve. He developed a plunger-pole pumping system, which was progress from the earlier inverted engine, and more efficient. He also invented machines for agriculture, including a threshing machine and a steam-powered cultivator.

All was going well when, in May 1813, he received a visit from a Peruvian businessman, Francisco Uville. He had a partnership in a silver mine high in the Andes at Cerro de Pasco, but progress now required a steam pumping system to get at the ore. At a height of nearly 15,000ft and only approachable by mule tracks, there was no way they could have got one of the massive Boulton & Watt engines up there, so he had come to Trevithick.

The Cornishman was happy to supply the engines and sent out the essential parts with a team of Cornish workers to install them. Things, however, did not go well in Peru and Trevithick decided that the only answer was to go and sort things out for himself. He had patented the plunger-pole pump and was happy that the royalties would be quite enough to keep his wife and family while he was away.

He left England in October 1816 for what should have been a short, but highly profitable visit. If the engines worked, he would have had a share in the silver extracted. He was successful but never got the silver. He had been vaguely aware of political dissent in South America but had not anticipated Simon Bolivar's army marching into Peru and taking over the mines. He was now stuck in Peru with no finances.

He spent the next few years on various schemes to regain the fortune that had been snatched away from him. Eventually, he formed a partnership with a Scotsman, James Gerard, to begin working a gold mine in Costa Rica. It was decided that they needed to raise capital in England.

They could have headed for the west coast, but they realised that to maximise their profits in trading with Europe, they would be better served by creating a connection from the mines to the east coast, where ships could be loaded and avoid the notoriously dangerous passage round Cape Horn. They decided to make their way east to establish where a new route could be made.

It proved a disastrous mistake, as everything went wrong – the raft they had been using was lost with most of their essentials, although they did eventually make it to the coast. Eventually, they made their way up the coast to Cartagena in Colombia, where there was one final accident. Trevithick was tipped out of a canoe and would have been attacked by an alligator had not a passerby shot the animal.

Trevithick was now in a desperate position, stuck in Cartagena without the funds to pay for a passage and faced only with the prospect of repeating his journey back to the mines. The next part of the story is almost incredible, and we must return to Britain to find out what had been happening in his absence.

In 1814, John Blenkinsop was the manager of Middleton Colliery, near Leeds, which relied on a horsedrawn tramway to take coal to the Aire & Calder Canal. The price of fodder had risen sharply, and he applied to buy the Trevithick patent – as Trevithick had, by then, given up on locomotives, he was happy to sell.

Blenkinsop was aware of the rail problem but had a solution – he could use a lightweight engine but increase the traction by using a rack-and-pinion system, whereby a cog on the engine engaged with a toothed rail laid alongside the track. It worked and other mine owners in the north sent their engineers to see this system. Among them was George Stephenson. He went on to build his own first engine, *Blücher*, which was closely based on the Middleton engine but without the rack and pinion.

Stephenson was to go on enthusiastically supporting steam locomotives when others had begun to falter, and when he was appointed chief engineer for the Stockton & Darlington Railway, he established a locomotive works in Newcastle under his son Robert's name. Robert may have been the name over the door, but George was very much in charge, so when Robert was offered the chance to go to South America to take charge of a mining project, he naturally grabbed the opportunity to visit that exotic continent.

While Robert was away, plans were put in hand for the most ambitious railway scheme to date, which would unite the port of Liverpool with the heartland of the thriving cotton industry, Manchester. It was to be run for both passengers and freight, but the question was – were the locomotives of the day capable of running such a system? There was an argument that it would be far better using a system of stationary engines to haul trains along by cable. The question was to be settled by a competition, and if anyone could meet the stringent conditions with a locomotive, the builders would not only get a cash prize but the far more important contract to build for the line.

The Stephenson Company was bound to take up the challenge, but George, whatever his virtues, was not the greatest mechanical engineer. An urgent message went out to South America to Robert to come home at once. He agreed and thus eventually found himself in Cartagena at the same time as Trevithick.

It is known that they met, but there is no record of their conversation. Samuel Smiles invented an unlikely one, but surely, given Robert's summons, locomotives must have been discussed. I like to think that Trevithick mentioned the advantage to be gained by the steam blast pipe, but that is pure speculation. We do know, however, that when Robert returned and began working on their entry for the competition, it was a vital element, together with the multi-tubular boiler that went into the locomotive that won the prize – one of the most famous locomotives in railway history, the *Rocket*.

Back in England, thanks to a generous loan from Stephenson to pay his fare, Trevithick settled briefly with his family, who had not seen him nor heard from him in over a decade. At the very end of his life, he made the sort of connection that would have been invaluable earlier – the support of a successful manufacturer, John Hall of Dartford. Their association was to be a short one. He died there on 22 April 1833. George Stephenson has rightly been hailed as the 'father of the railways', for his promotion of the system, but Richard Trevithick was unquestionably the 'father of the locomotive'.

6

ISAMBARD KINGDOM BRUNEL

A famous engineer, but included here as the designer of the first ocean-going steamer to be built with an iron hull and driven by a screw propeller.

Brunel is perhaps best known for his role as chief engineer for the Great Western Railway (GWR), but in that role, he made no real impact on transport history. It is true that his broad-gauge line was unlike any other being built at the time, but it ultimately had to give way to the narrower Stephenson-gauge lines. This does not necessarily mean that one was better than the other, but it made little sense to have two mainline gauges in one small country. It was a situation that would cause many problems when they met up, involving transferring goods and passengers from one system to the other. To change everything to broad gauge would have been ruinously expensive, with stations, viaducts and tunnels all having to be rebuilt to take the extra width.

Brunel's strength lay in the civil engineering of the lines – when it came to the mechanical-engineering side, he proved to be a good deal less successful. His original specifications for the GWR caused the engineers endless headaches trying to make locomotives fit his demands. It was only when he employed Daniel Gooch as chief mechanical engineer that the GWR began to get successful engines. So, in this chapter, we shall be looking almost exclusively at his contribution to the world of shipping.

Isambard's father, Marc, was French and served for a time in the French Navy, but with outspoken royalist views, he was forced into hiding during the French Revolution. At the same time, he met a young Cornish woman, Sophie Kingdom, who had been studying English in France and was equally caught up in the Revolution. Marc managed to make his escape and made his way to the United States, where he had a successful career as an engineer, but eventually he took the opportunity to go to England. There, he was to make his own contribution to maritime history by designing machinery for making blocks for the navy's sailing ships. He was reunited with Sophie Kingdom, they married, and Isambard was born in 1806.

From the first, his father was determined that he should have a practical as well as a theoretical education, and he was sent off to an apprenticeship with a leading instrument-maker in Paris. By the age of 18, Isambard was working with his father.

Marc had acquired a contract for a second attempt to construct a tunnel under the Thames. Things were going well until May 1827, when, just as had happened to Trevithick's attempt, the works were inundated, and everything came to a halt. Eventually, work would be resumed and the tunnel completed, but for the time being, both Brunels were unemployed.

Isambard Kingdom Brunel. (J.C. Horsley, engraved by T.O. Barlow; *The Life of Isambard Kingdom Brunel, Civil Engineer* by Isambard Brunel Junior [1870])

Two possible projects appeared almost simultaneously: one for a bridge over the River Vistula in Poland, the other over the River Avon at Bristol. Inevitably, the more prestigious of the two for a European capital was taken by the father, leaving Isambard to make his way to Bristol, a decision that was to have a profound effect on the young man's career.

The design of the bridge over the gorge at Clifton was to be decided by a competition judged by a committee headed by the eminent engineer Thomas Telford. Brunel's proposal called for towers on the top of the cliffs bordering the gorge, joined by a suspension bridge. Telford, however, had built a suspension bridge over the Menai Straits and had experienced difficulties in stabilising it, which convinced him that he had reached the limit at which a bridge would be safe. As the Brunel proposal called for a far greater span, it was rejected. With no other viable proposal appearing, Telford produced his own design. To shorten the span, the suspension section was attached to two Gothic towers built on the riverbank. It was considered grotesque and the committee decided to overrule Telford and Brunel was appointed.

Work began, but the money ran out with only the towers built, and the bridge would not be completed in Brunel's lifetime. But the citizens of Bristol were very impressed by the young engineer, and he was engaged in another project to improve the harbour, a job for which he designed a small steamboat that was moved by chains backwards and forwards using a metal plate to scrape the bottom of the harbour.

When proposals were made in 1832 for a railway from Bristol to London, the company appointed Brunel to work as their engineer. At one meeting, a member of the GWR board expressed doubts about the wisdom of building such a long line – far longer than any other in hand at the time. Brunel, with typical bravado, famously said that it was not a problem and added that he saw no reason to stop there – why not go to New York as well?

Whether he meant it to be taken seriously or not, one of the board, Thomas Guppy, did. A company was formed to develop the idea, with Brunel and Guppy being joined by a former sea captain who was then in charge of the Bristol Quays, Christopher Claxton. It was to become the Great Western Steamship Company.

The general view at the time was that it was impossible for steamers to undertake such a long voyage, as they would run out of fuel somewhere in the middle of the Atlantic. Dr Dionysius Lardner was acclaimed as an eminent scientist, but his 'scientific' views on Brunel projects were anything but. About the GWR project, he alarmed the public by warning them that if a train passing through Box Tunnel was on the downward slope and got out of control, it could reach a speed of 100mph, which no living being could survive. Apart from the obvious fact that we regularly do survive greater speeds, he had, as Brunel pointed out, not allowed for air resistance. Now, he gave his considered opinion that it would never be possible for a steamer to cross the Atlantic using steam power alone. Doubling the size of a vessel would not help because it would need twice as much fuel – a bit of a schoolboy howler.

As Archimedes pointed out, a floating body displaces its own weight of liquid, so in moving that body through water, it must overcome water resistance and – to a far less extent – air resistance, and that depends on the area in contact and not the volume. To take a simple example: supposing you wanted to push a cube through water. The resistance would be the force pushing against the face of the cube. If the cube had 1ft sides, each would measure 1ft^2 and the volume would be 1ft^3 – double everything and the face would be 4ft^2 but the volume would be 8ft^3. For ships, big really would be better.

The ship to be known as *Great Western* was built at the Patterson Yard in Bristol and work got under way on what would be probably the largest wooden vessel yet constructed. Designed to carry 128 passengers with extra accommodation for their servants, the centrepiece was the magnificent public room, decorated with fifty large painted panels. The engine was to be built in London by the established company Maudslay, Sons & Field and was to be a side-lever engine. This can best be described as rather like an early beam engine, except that the pivoting beam is at the bottom of the engine, not the top. When the work on the ship was completed, it was towed down to London to have the engines installed.

Meanwhile, the British & American Steam Navigation Company had been formed with the same ambition of being the first to cross the Atlantic. Their vessel was being built in London but the Scottish company supplying the engine had gone bankrupt. There were going to be huge delays in getting the ship ready, so they were dismayed to find the imposing *Great Western* being towed up the Thames. If they were to claim the prize, they needed a ship quickly, and they purchased *Sirius*. It was 700 tons compared to the 1,340 tons of the Brunel vessel, but it was a working ship.

As *Great Western* set out on its sea trials in March 1838, *Sirius* was also under steam – not on a trial but starting out for Cork to take on fuel for her voyage to New York. This might not have been a problem but shortly after *Great Western* set out for Bristol there was a fire in the forward boiler room. The crew, led by Captain Claxton, were dealing with the fire, when Brunel decided to go down to the boiler room himself, but the heat had damaged the ladder, a rung gave way, and he fell. Fortunately for him, he landed on top of the captain but he was injured and quite incapable of carrying on with the voyage.

He was put ashore, and the ship continued to Bristol for her crossing. It left on 7 April, but *Sirius* was already under way, having left on the 4th – and on a shorter crossing, equivalent to a full day's sailing time. *Great Western* steadily gained on its rival, but it was *Sirius* that arrived first in New York by a few hours.

It was galling for the *Great Western* team, but Brunel's point had been made. The smaller vessel had arrived with her bunkers virtually empty – it was even rumoured that the crew had resorted to tearing off cabin doors to feed the boiler for the last few miles. *Great Western*, however, still had ample supplies of coal left – Brunel was right, when it came to Atlantic crossings, big really was best.

However, there was now a new problem: Brunel could not build a bigger ship using traditional wooden planking. Fortunately, there was a solution already available. The ironmaster John Wilkinson had built a barge with an iron hull that was successfully launched on the River Severn in 1787. Other iron-hulled vessels followed, and Brunel decided that iron was the answer for the new ship.

The job of designing the engine went to the engineer Francis Humphreys, who was working at Hall's of Dartford – the company with which Trevithick had worked in his last years. He designed a trunk engine, one in which the piston rod was a hollow cylinder and the connection from the crank passed inside the tube to the piston itself. It was assumed that Hall's would build the engine, but they declined, so the Great Western Company established their own engineering works.

They hit an immediate problem. Forging was still carried out using various types of water-powered tilt hammers, and it was proving almost impossible to forge the huge crankshaft the new engine required. The tilt hammer head could not be raised high enough.

The problem was sent to the engineer James Nasmyth, who promptly came up with a solution – the steam hammer. The hammer head would be lifted vertically by steam power and then allowed to fall back down onto the iron on the anvil. It was a huge improvement on earlier devices and steam hammers became fixtures in shipyards around the world.

All was going well until Brunel heard of another invention. If the paddle steamer's wheel could be thought of as a waterwheel working in reverse, then there was another device that might be adaptable, one that had been around for centuries – the Archimedean screw. Basically, this consists of a helical screw set inside a closely fitting cylinder. If the device has one end dipped below the water level and the screw is turned, water will be drawn up the tube.

It was a farmer, Francis Pettit Smith, who recognised that a helical screw might be used for propulsion. His first experiments with clockwork model boats on a pond at his farm were initially unpromising. Then the long screw was broken, and he discovered that the system worked best with a single turn – he named this a 'propeller'. From the pond, he moved on to an experimental craft and eventually, he installed a steam engine in a former schooner, fitted a propeller and sent the vessel, *Archimedes*, on a demonstration voyage round Britain.

Thomas Guppy set off to see the vessel and reported back favourably. The decision was taken to abandon the paddle wheels in favour of the screw propeller. This meant abandoning the Humphreys engine – and that troublesome crankshaft would no longer be needed.

The first stage in building the new ship was to lay down the lines, work which was carried out by Patterson, but with contributions from others, including Isambard's father, Marc Brunel, who used models to test the design. The outstanding

The author beside the replica propeller of SS *Great Britain*, during the filming of the TV series *Big, Bigger, Biggest*.

A model of the engine of *Great Britain*, held in the Victoria & Albert Museum. (E. Keble Chatterton, *Steamships and Their Story* [Cassell and Company Ltd, 1910])

feature of the hull was the design of the bows, known as 'clipper lines', which were slightly hollow, giving very fine lines. It was to be 274ft on the keel with a breadth of 50ft 6in, the latter determined by the need to get through the entrance locks at the Bristol floating harbour. The plating of the hull was akin to that of a clinker-built wooden ship, with lines of plates overlapping rather than meeting edge on.

With the decision to use the propeller, a new engine was needed, and this was based on a design patented by Marc Brunel, the 'triangular engine'. The steam cylinders were angled up at 60 degrees, each 88in diameter. They operated on a massive overhead crankshaft, from which the drive was transmitted to the propeller shaft by four chains. The steam was at very low pressure – an average of just 5psi. The vessel also carried fore-and-aft sails on five masts. The accommodation for passengers included both a dining saloon and a promenade saloon for first-class passengers, but the actual cabins were quite small, usually about 6ft wide.

In 1845, SS *Great Britain* underwent sea trials that went well, although off Lundy in the Bristol Channel, it was hit by two immense waves that brought the vessel to a momentary standstill but caused no serious damage. In July 1845, it left for its first voyage to the United States and embarrassingly missed the approach to New York Harbour.

A far worse error occurred when *Great Britain* left Liverpool in September 1846. The course should have taken it to the north of the Isle of Man, then round the north coast of Ireland. Quite how such a gross navigational error could have happened remains a mystery, but they went south of the island and instead of rounding the Irish coast ran straight into it at Dundrum Bay in County Down. The ship was eventually salvaged and towed back to Liverpool for repairs. The company's coffers did not contain the funds for the necessary work, and the ship that had cost an estimated £22,000 to build was eventually bought for just £17,000.

Great Britain was to continue in service until 1886, when it was caught in a fierce storm when rounding Cape Horn and, like many other ships caught in such conditions, headed for the safety of Stanley Harbour in the Falklands. It was decided that the damage was too great to be worth the cost of repair and it was decided to use it as a floating wool store.

By 1936, *Great Britain* was considered too unsafe and was towed round to Sparrow Cove, where it was abandoned. There it languished until 1970, when it was floated onto a pontoon to be towed back to Bristol and the dry dock in which it was built. Since then, it has been fully restored, though the replica engine no longer relies on steam to be demonstrated to visitors.

The first-class dining saloon on SS *Great Britain*. (The Wub, CCA SA 40 via Wikimedia Commons)

SS *Great Britain*, fully restored and returned to the Bristol dock where she was built. (Author)

Unlike the other inventions discussed so far, Brunel's is perhaps rather different, in that he never actually invented any part of this historic vessel himself. What makes his story special, however, is his ability to see beyond accepted opinion. He saw that big ships were the answer; that they needed to be built of iron not wood and the propeller was more effective for ocean travel than paddle wheels.

Ever since the success of *Great Britain*, the shipping world has been dominated by iron, screw-propelled vessels – and they have continued getting bigger. Brunel was to go on to build one even larger ship, the *Great Eastern*, intended for trade with Australia, but his life was nearly over. He died on 5 September 1859. For many, he is associated mainly with the GWR, but apart from querying the standard gauge then in use, he made few real innovations. It is his role in revolutionising ship building that has earned him a well-deserved place in this book.

7

Ernst Werner von Siemens

> *An electrical engineer who designed both the first electric tram and the first electric railway locomotive.*

In this chapter, we are leaving behind the steam age to enter the new world of electric power, but before turning to the subject himself, we need to step back to look at the history of electricity.

Early experiments were chiefly concerned with what was known as 'static' electricity – the kind that's often produced at children's parties when a balloon is rubbed on someone's hair and then floats up to the ceiling and sticks there. Various devices using friction were developed to make electricity in this way.

A different approach was taken by Professor of Physics Alessandro Volta at Pavia University in Italy. He famously discovered that an electric current would make the legs of dead frogs twitch. This led him to look for new ways to produce electricity and in 1799 he found the answer. He built up a pile of alternating silver and zinc discs separated by cardboard soaked in brine. If the two ends were connected by a wire, then electricity would flow through it. The device that, in effect, stored electricity was known as a 'voltaic pile' – and the name gave us the standard unit of electricity, the volt. It was the forerunner of the modern battery.

Electricity was available, but no one had yet thought of using it in transport. That had to wait for another development.

Michael Faraday was an unlikely candidate for a scientific career. The son of a blacksmith, he began his working life running errands for a London bookseller and binder, George Ribeau. He was allowed to browse the books in the shop, and it was when reading a copy of *Encyclopaedia Britannica* that was waiting to be bound that he became interested in science and electricity in particular. He joined the City Philosophical Society, where young working men gathered to talk about science and listen to lectures. Ribeau was impressed by his enthusiasm and managed to arrange for Faraday to have tickets for a series of lectures given by the eminent scientist, Humphry Davy at the Royal Institution. The young man was now desperate to abandon bookbinding for a scientific career, but with no formal qualification, he found it all but impossible.

Then an opportunity arrived, when Davy had to sack his assistant for drunkenness and took Faraday on. He toured Europe with Davy and gradually developed a reputation for himself as a highly competent scientist in his own right. His big moment came in 1821, when the journal *Annals of Philosophy* commissioned him to write an article on recent discoveries made by the Danish scientist Hans Christian Oersted. He had discovered there was a connection between electricity and magnetism – if a compass needle was held near a wire with a current running through it, the needle would deflect towards the wire.

Faraday not only read Oersted's reports on the phenomenon but he repeated the experiments for himself. He discovered that a wire carrying a current would move in a circle round a fixed magnet. He was later to demonstrate that the converse was true – a magnet moving round a fixed wire would induce a current. The first experiment demonstrated the basis for the electric motor, the latter, the electric generator. He gave his first demonstration of the correlation between electricity and magnetism at a Royal Society meeting in 1824.

Thanks to his work, Faraday, the blacksmith's son, was eventually made a Fellow of the Royal Society – in spite of objections by his former employer, Davy. No one outside the scientific community seemed especially interested in this new phenomenon or saw any practical application. When asked by a famous politician what use this electricity was, Faraday gave the sort of answer designed to appeal to any politician – 'one day you may be able to tax it'.

But we are now closer to the world of transport – for, in theory if not in practice, Faraday's generator and motor could be put to practical use. So, it is time to start the story of Ernst Werner Siemens, who had not yet earned the title 'von'.

He was born in the village of Lenthe, near Hamburg, in what was then Prussia, in 1816. His father was a tenant farmer and he was the fifth child to be born – they were to be followed by three more. In 1823, the lease on the farm ran out and was not renewed, so the family had to move to a new farm in Menzendorf in Lower Saxony. In his early years, Werner was taught by his grandmother but at the age of 11 he went to a secondary school in Schönberg, some 6km away. He was only there for one year before his father engaged a private tutor.

Then, at 15, he and his brother Hans were sent to a secondary school in Lübeck. At school, he showed a real interest in mathematics, but the family were struggling financially,

Ernst Werner von Siemens.

and he was forced to leave. Ideally, he would have gone on to university, but that was out of the question. There was, however, an alternative that would give him an education in science and technology – he joined the army as an officer cadet.

He started off in the artillery, but in 1835, he transferred to study at the artillery and engineering school, where he attended classes in chemistry, physics and mathematics. By the summer of 1837, he had gained his commission as a second lieutenant.

The following years put a great deal of strain on the young man. In 1839, both his parents died. The family had steadily grown and now there were ten young children left parentless. He was now the eldest son with responsibility for the family, with an elder brother having been disinherited. He used his time in the army to increase his scientific knowledge to try to develop projects that might show a profit.

His first effort was a method of gilding silver-nickel objects by electrolysis – his first step into the world of electricity. He gained a patent in 1842. Things were going well, but this was a time when duelling was still common, although illegal – a duelling scar was regarded as a mark of honour. Siemens was involved in several, which were studiously ignored by the authorities. But on one occasion, when he was acting as a second, he was reported and faced a court martial. He was sentenced to three years' imprisonment – the law had been upheld. But within three weeks he had been officially pardoned, and in October 1842, he was appointed to the artillery workshop in Berlin.

He now needed to find a way to make money from his patent. He went into an informal partnership with his 20-year-old brother, who sailed to England in 1843, where he sold the rights to the gilding process to the Birmingham silversmith

George Richards Elkington, who was later to become one of the country's leading specialists in electroplated silver.

The success of Siemens' first invention encouraged him to look at other uses of electricity, and he began to look at the electric telegraph. This worked by deflecting a magnetic needle when an electric current flowed near it. Early experiments by Baron Schilling began in 1822 but he seemed to have made little attempt to develop the idea commercially. However, news of his experiments were passed to William Fothergill Cooke, who recognised that such a device would be invaluable for railway signalling, enabling distant signal boxes to pass on information about train movements to each other. Cooke had initial difficulties but joined forces with Professor Charles Wheatstone of King's College, London to perfect a working machine. They installed a double-needle version for the Great Western Railway line between Slough and Paddington. It was used to send coded messages.

Siemens was convinced he could improve on this and developed his pointer telegraph. The two ends of the telegraph contained identical transmitters with synchronised rotating pointers. If an operator pressed a key, the current was interrupted and both pointers stopped at identical letters.

Siemens was still in the army and now needed a partner to develop his invention and he was recommended to a skilled mechanic, Johann Georg Halske. They began manufacturing in Berlin. In 1848, they acquired a contract for supplying telegraphic equipment for two routes from Berlin to Frankfurt am Main and to Aachen. The connecting cables were insulated with what was then a comparatively unknown material, gutta-percha.

In 1849, the telegraph line between Berlin and Frankfurt was opened. However, there were problems, and the Prussian state refused to give the young company further orders. With

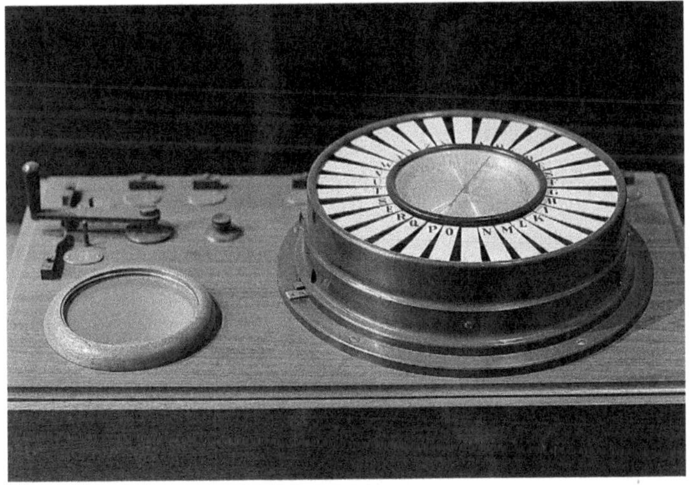

The Siemens pointer telegraph held in the Übersee-Museum, Bremen. (Bin im Garten, CCA SA 3.0 via Wikimedia Commons)

his brother Carl settled in St Petersburg, Siemens was able to obtain a highly lucrative contract to supply telegraph equipment to Russia and shortly afterwards, telegraph contracts were resumed in Prussia. An even more ambitious project was undertaken when, in 1865, they acquired the contract to build a telegraph line from England to India, which was followed by a link from Europe to America.

While the company was busily engaged with telegraph projects, Siemens was already pursuing a new idea. We are now back with the electric dynamo, which had originally been developed as an idea in the 1850s by Anianus Jedlick in Hungary and Søren Hjorth in Denmark, but neither had attempted to put it into production.

Siemens' first attempt was based on a double armature and a permanent magnet, but was only able to produce a low voltage because of the comparatively weak magnetic field. He noticed that there was residual magnetism in the soft iron core and that the low voltage could be used to power the electromagnets. It was an idea that came to be known as 'self-excitation of electricity'. He could dispense with batteries and permanent magnets altogether.

Siemens went on to develop a dynamo that could be used to power electric lights. In 1879, he demonstrated the electric lighting system for his own home in Charlottenburg and invited 250 guests to admire it – and, it was hoped, spread the word. At the same time, he was also looking at a new use for his dynamo, uniting it with an electric motor.

Shortly afterwards, he introduced the world to a new use of electricity. In 1879, Berlin was staging a commercial fair, and it was here that Siemens laid down a narrow-gauge

An early example of a Siemens dynamo, dating from 1873. (Bin im Garten/ Wellcome Library, London, CCA 4.0 via Wikimedia Commons)

track on which he ran a train hauled by a small electric locomotive – the first of its kind. Passengers were given rides, but the idea was to promote his plan for a high-level electric railway to run above Friedrichstrasse, one of the main streets of the capital. Unfortunately, the plans were blocked by the Kaiser.

Undaunted, Siemens turned instead to developing an electric streetcar in the Lichterfelde district. Ironically, Berlin does now have an overhead electric rail system, the S-Bahn, which has an extensive network of 340km.

In 1883, Siemens and Halske provided the machinery for a tram for a consortium in Frankfurt am Main to run from there to Offenbach, 6.7km away. A powerplant was built to

The original electric locomotive with a trainload of passengers at the Berlin Trade Exhibition of 1879.

supply the electricity and the line opened in 1884. The trams consisted of two cars, of which only the leading car was powered. The overhead cables were encased in slotted gas piping, with a lug passing through which was attached to the tram. It was the world's first electric tram. Within a period of just four years, he had built the first electric railway and the first electric streetcar and tram.

That is not the end of the story. Magnus Volk lived in Brighton and was an early enthusiast of electric lighting, which he installed in his own home in 1870. Siemens had been suspicious of depending on electric lighting as a source of profit because of the expense. He was convinced it would only be used for very rich people or for very prestigious buildings.

No building in Brighton was more prestigious than the Royal Pavilion and Volk got a contract to supply lighting. He used a Siemens dynamo, which was powered by a gas engine – an early form of internal combustion engine where the fuel was gas instead of petrol or diesel. When Brighton Council took over the electric supply, he found himself with a surplus generator and a small electric motor. Siemens had demonstrated his locomotive in London and Volk had been impressed. He now got permission to build an electric railway along the seafront. It was a 2ft 8½in gauge and the Siemens dynamo produced electricity at 40 amps and 60 volts to drive a 6hp engine, taking its power from the rails. It ran at a stately 10 mph but proved very popular and Volk's Electric Railway still runs in Brighton today, as it did more than a century ago.

This was Britain's first electric railway but there was no rush to extend electrification to mainline rail services. Steam still ruled and the cost of creating the infrastructure was considered unjustifiable. There was, however, one notable exception – the London Underground. The use of steam

The electric tramway at Frankfurt am Main, which opened in 1873.
(Wood engraving after a sketch by A. Sänger, *c.* 1885)

Volk's Electric Railway running along the seafront at Brighton.
(Peter Trimming)

ISLAND PLATFORM AT STOCKWELL STATION, CITY AND SOUTH LONDON RAILWAY

The City & South London Railway – the first section of the tube system to be electrified. (duncan1890 via iStock)

trains underground had never been entirely satisfactory, despite various attempts to reduce the fumes. Electricity provided the ideal solution.

The first to electrify was the City & South London line, but to do so, they had to build their own power station – a huge scaling up from the little Volk line. Here, three 450hp steam engines were used to turn three generators, each weighing in at 17 tons. They supplied a DC current to a third rail at 450 amps and 500 volts. This was enough to power a train of three carriages. This was soon followed by other parts of the system being electrified – an example that would eventually be followed by underground and metro systems around the world.

Siemens was not merely concerned with his business; he was a keen advocate for introducing scientific research to his homeland and in 1883, he offered the government a plot of land near his home in Charlottenburg worth 300,000 marks, roughly 150,000 euros at today's prices, for the construction of a scientific institute. It was not until 1887 that it agreed to accept the offer and develop the Imperial Physics & Technical Institute.

His efforts were recognised by Kaiser Friedrich III, who raised him into the nobility and Werner Siemens became Werner von Siemens. It was not an honour he had requested, nor one he particularly wanted, but no one had bothered to ask him if he wanted it. He apparently only discovered he had received the honour when he read about it in the paper. He was quite annoyed but felt he could not refuse it.

It was an initiative that played a part in developing Prussia, and later Germany, into a leading industrial and scientific nation. Siemens finally gave up being head of the company in 1890 at the age of 74 and died two years later. He left behind a highly successful family business that developed over the years and remains a leading industrial company as Siemens AG. He also left behind a transport world that had been transformed by electricity.

8

KARL BENZ AND GOTTLIEB DAIMLER

The two German engineers listed jointly as designers of the first motor car and first motorcycle.

Steam power had dominated transport in the nineteenth century, but an alternative was to be developed in the latter years, the internal combustion engine. The first practical version was invented by Nicolaus Otto, a German engineer, in 1878. The fuel was gas, and the engine used the four-stroke system first mentioned by a Frenchman, Alphonse Beau de Rochas – although it is unlikely Otto had ever heard of his work. In the first stroke, the gas is drawn into the cylinder, in the second, it is compressed, the third stroke ignites it and on the fourth, the burnt gases are exhausted.

Otto engines became popular as alternatives to steam engines as there was no longer anyone needed to keep stoking a boiler – it had simply to be connected to a gas supply, which was by then readily available from a town's gasworks. It was not, however, useful in the world of transport because the gas engine was anchored to its supply. That had to wait for a suitable fuel to be available.

The first experiments using some type of oil as a fuel were made in Vienna in 1873. The most successful of the early engines using heavy oil was designed by William Dent Priestman in 1886, working on the Otto four-stroke cycle. Air was compressed by a pump and stored in a reservoir. The compressed air was used to spray the oil into a vaporiser heated by the exhaust gas. More air was added to make the explosive mixture.

The engine was useful in places where no gas supply was available and in 1889, a portable version was demonstrated. The next step, which will be the subject of this chapter, was to make such an engine drive a vehicle.

There are two names in the title of this chapter, simply because Benz and Daimler both worked at the same time and both contributed to the development of motor transport. We shall be looking at Benz first, as he was the originator of a motor car just before Daimler demonstrated his motorcycle.

Karl Benz was born in 1844 in the little village of Pfaffenrot, near Karlsruhe in the Black Forest. His family had traditionally been the village blacksmiths, but his father was fascinated by the railway that was being built through the village, linking Karlsruhe to Heidelberg, and managed to get a job at the locomotive works, leaving his brother to take over the forge. He eventually achieved his ambition of becoming an engine driver, but in 1846, he was involved in an accident when a train derailed. He helped to manually get the engine back on the line before, covered in sweat, he rejoined his own locomotive and spent the day on the open footplate. Within a few days, he had suffered a severe chill, and shortly afterwards, he died from what was probably pneumonia. His wife was left a widow with a 2-year-old son.

Karl Benz.

At the age of 9, Karl went to school at Karlsruhe, where he immediately showed a flair for science and all things practical. He was clearly an inventive boy and when he managed to get hold of a camera, he toured the local villages taking photos of the locals, for which he charged them a small fee, which must have helped the family finances. At the age of 17, he left school for the Karlsruhe Polytechnic to study engineering. One of his major influences there was the head of the college, Professor Rechtenbacher, who held the view that, despite the success of the steam-powered railways and road vehicles, the future lay with lighter engines – but he never specified what those engines might be.

After four years at college, Benz joined an engineering firm in Karlsruhe, but in what little spare time he had he began working on ideas for a road vehicle that would not be powered by steam. To get more experience, he joined a manufacturer of cranes and pumps in Mannheim, where he got to work in the drawing office. It seems that an accident gave him fresh impetus, not to himself, but to a man known to us only as Walter, an enthusiastic walker who had developed a problem that prevented him from getting around as he had used to do.

Walter bought a hobby horse, a primitive form of bicycle, which had no pedals, but supported the rider, while he propelled himself around using his feet on the ground. He was quite unable to make it work and it was passed on to his friend, Karl Benz, who set about improving it. He was soon able to make trips on the unwieldy device, and it rekindled his interest in motive powers – although he felt that the bicycle was too unstable to be the basis for a powered machine.

Karl's next move was to a bridge-building firm in Pforzheim and it was while he was there that he met Berta Ringer, who he married in 1872. She was destined to have her own special place in motoring history. By then, he had already decided that if he was ever to see his plans for a motorised vehicle realised, he would need to have his own business, and so he used his savings to rent a workshop in Mannheim. He developed a small two-stroke gas engine, but funds and work had run out.

Rescue appeared in the shape of a photographer named Bühler, who commissioned Benz to provide him with highly polished steel plates. He was impressed by the result and offered to put money into Benz's business. This enabled the engineer to work on more gas engines, and they were sufficiently successful for the Benz workshop to become a limited company – Mannheim Gas Engine Co.

Now, it seemed, was the time for Benz to develop his original idea of a motor vehicle with an internal combustion engine, but the other partners absolutely refused to authorise any development money – they were doing far too well with the gas engine. He abandoned the partnership and returned to his original workshop but now he acquired a new partner, Mannheim merchant Max Rose, who while not exactly an enthusiast for the idea of developing a motor car, would not oppose it.

Benz recognised that he would need a light engine, and his single-cylinder petrol engine would only have slightly more than 100mm bore. Previous internal combustion engines had been run at 120–130rpm, but to increase power, this was increased to 250–300rpm. He designed it to work on the Otto four-stroke cycle. He decided that he would use electric ignition, based on a battery, an induction coil and a commutator in the form of a rotary switch, which, when contact was made, induced the spark. This turned out not to work very well, so the battery was replaced by a dynamo, turned by a belt fitted into a groove on the engine's flywheel. The engine itself was under the rear of the car, with the cylinder set horizontally. He devised a form of float-carburettor, in which the fuel and air could be mixed, with the float controlling the amount of fuel entering the chamber.

When it came to building the car itself, weight was always a concern, so the wheels were made with wire spokes, supplied by a bicycle manufacturer. The car had large rear wheels, which were sprung, and the steering was via a steering column to the smaller unsprung front wheel. The frame was tubular, with padded seats for the driver and passenger. The crankshaft was vertical, at the end of which was a pair of bevel gears to a horizontal shaft that led via a belt to a countershaft with a differential gear low down in the car from which there were chain drives to the rear wheels. The belt could be moved to a loose pulley to allow the engine to be run without the car moving – a device that Benz would have been familiar with

The first Benz motor car.

from his workshop days when similar devices were used for machine tools worked from overhead line shafting.

It was given its first trial in 1885 in front of a crowd of interested spectators. The flywheel was swung, the engine started – and the proud inventor was so delighted he forgot about steering and ran into a brick wall. The next run was not advertised, but once again there was a problem, this time with the belt. Gradually, the problems were solved and greater distances covered.

The car trundled along at around 8mph, which was not exactly speedy, but it was the world's first motor car and had proved that the concept worked. It now attracted the attention of the press, who had yet to come up with the name 'motor car'. A report appeared in the *Neue Badische Landeszeitung* of 4 June 1886, 'There is no doubt that this motorized-velocipede will soon attract a large number of friends since it can be expected that it will prove to be extremely practical and useful for doctors, travellers, sportsmen and others'.

The trials could now be followed up with a period of development. The first changes represented major improvements. The 1hp car with a single gear was transformed into a 3hp with two gears and the springing was improved. He exhibited a vehicle at the Munich Imperial Exhibition of 1888, where it took a great deal of persuasion before the police would allow him to run the vehicle on public roads, but he was rewarded for his perseverance by the award of the Exhibition's gold medal. He was, however, still reluctant to take any vehicle out on long-distance runs – and certainly had no intention of allowing his family to try to do so. They, however, had other ideas.

The Benzes' two sons, though only 13 and 15 years old, had both learned to drive, and now they plotted an adventure. They had heard that their mother wanted to visit relatives at

Pforzheim, 57 miles away. They persuaded her to let them drive her there without telling her husband. On a summer day in 1888, while Benz was still in bed, they left, leaving a note behind telling him where they were going.

Things went well as far as Heidelberg, but when they reached the hills things became more difficult – going uphill, the younger brother, Eugen, took control and Richard and his mother got out to help push the vehicle. Going downhill presented a different problem. The leather facing on the brakes kept shredding and stops had to be made at various cobblers for fresh leather covering to be put in place. Then there were problems with the driving chains that required the handiwork of local blacksmiths for repairs.

Frau Benz proved to be far more than just a passenger and occasional pusher. When the flow of fuel to the carburettor stopped, she removed the obstacle with her hatpin, and later, the ignition wires short-circuited, so she removed one of her garters to provide new insulation.

They finally reached Pforzheim in the evening and tele-graphed Benz to tell him the journey had been a success and all were safe and well. It had a practical value as well – it con-vinced Benz that he probably needed a third gear.

Benz built only three three-wheeled vehicles, before turn-ing to a four-wheeled design in 1893. The main difference between that and the earlier cars was that the crankshaft was now horizontal instead of vertical and there was a two-speed belt drive. It was a great success and hundreds of models of this 3½hp vehicle were sold. Benz was well set on a successful business career as a car manufacturer.

We can now look at the career of his fellow pioneer, Gottlieb Daimler. He was born in 1834 at Schorndorf, to the east of Stuttgart, where his father was a baker. He had ambi-tions for the boy and hoped he would be able to get a suitable

Karl and Berta Benz. (Fronteras, CCA SA 4.0 via Wikimedia Commons)

Gottlieb Daimler.

office job in local government, so Gottlieb was sent to the German equivalent of a grammar school.

It soon became clear, however, that he was far more interested in practical matters than in the academic, and in 1848 he left school to take up an apprenticeship with a local master gunmaker, Hermann Reithel. Gottlieb showed himself to be both conscientious and skilled. Among his apprentice pieces were a pair of double-barrelled pistols with walnut butts, which he had beautifully carved. Reithel would have liked to keep Daimler on at the end of his apprenticeship, but he moved instead to work for another gunsmith named Wilke. When Wilke was appointed gunsmith to the court, he moved to Stuttgart and Daimler went with him. It marked an important turning point in his life.

Daimler began to realise that the trade of the gunsmith was not for him, and he managed to get a job at the engineering company Werkzeugmaschinenfabrik, at Grafenstadt, which also ran a training college. By 1857, he had saved enough money to study full time at the Stuttgart School for Advanced Training in the Industrial Arts, where he remained for two years, before returning for a time to Grafenstadt.

He was fortunate to have been befriended by Dr Steinbeis, who was an enthusiast for developing Germany's industrial life and helped promising young engineers to go abroad to see the latest developments. With his help, Daimler was able to travel, first to England, where he visited Sir Joseph Whitworth's works at Coventry, probably the most advanced engineering works in Europe at the time. He went on to Beyer Peacock in Manchester, which was famous for developing articulated steam locomotives. His engineering travels also took him to France and Belgium.

On returning to Germany, he worked for several companies before being offered the job of technical director at the

Karlsruhe engineering works, where he remained for five years. During his time there, he met and married Emma Kurtz, and they would have five children.

His next move was the most important of all. Nicolaus Otto had entered a partnership with Eugen Langen to form the NA Otto Company in Cologne, the first in the world to be set up for the manufacture of internal combustion engines. In 1872, they moved to larger premises and renamed the company Gasmotorenfabrik Deutz.

Daimler was recruited as technical director and was to continue working there for the next ten years. During that time, he brought in Wilhelm Maybach, who he had known as an apprentice at Reutlingen, as chief designer. The gas engine developed rapidly during his time there, with the first 100hp engine being produced. However, differences arose between Daimler and Otto, centred originally on the ignition system for the gas engines, which was only suitable for comparatively slow engines. Daimler was keen to develop internal combustion engines for transport, but the company was not willing to support the experiments. The differences made it difficult for Otto and Daimler to work together, so his only option if he was to develop his own ideas was to leave the company.

Daimler moved to a house in Cannstatt in 1882, which had a large summer house, to which he attached a workshop, where he and Maybach began working on their first experimental engine, known as the 'grandfather clock'. The old workshop has been preserved as a museum – and incidentally, it was only when visiting it some years ago that I discovered that our anglicised pronunciation of his name is wrong: the first syllable is pronounced 'dime' not 'dame'.

They often worked late into the night, and neighbours decided that they were certainly forging false coins and informed the police. One night, armed police arrived demanding admission, but fortunately the two inventors were able to convince them that their work was quite legitimate. The engine itself was a horizontal, air-cooled, single cylinder with a cast-iron flywheel, working at 900rpm. The second engine was similar but with an enclosed crankshaft and it was this engine that was installed in a motorcycle in 1886. The machine was mounted vertically between the two wheels, with the drive to the rear wheel via a leather band. There was an arrangement by which, when the brakes were applied, the band automatically slackened. Hot-tube ignition was used, in which the hot tube itself was heated red hot by a flame. There were small, stabilising wheels to either side, which could be raised up. The bicycle itself was still new at this time and no doubt the stabilisers were reassuring for anyone trying to ride a motorcycle – much as small children have similar devices on their own first bikes until they become confident.

There is some doubt about whether the motorcycle was ever ridden, but Daimler did not consider going into production. Now that the engine worked, he moved on to four-wheeled vehicles. He also tried the engine in a small boat on the River Neckar, but the idea was not well received. He then tried to experiment with using an engine to power an airship, but the attempt was not a success. Daimler and Maybach now concentrated on their much more successful business as builders of motor cars and in 1890, the Daimler motor company was formed.

For a time, both Daimler and Maybach left the company to work on their own development programmes, but rejoined in 1895, when Maybach took on the role of technical director. Wealthy car owners developed the new sport of motor-racing, and in 1894, the Paris–Rouen–Paris race was won by a car with a Daimler engine at an average speed of over 20km/h, which was impressive at the time.

The original Daimler motorcycle in the Mercedes-Benz Museum, Stuttgart. (Wladyslaw, CC A SA 2.0 via Wikimedia Commons)

This greatly impressed a wealthy Parisian banker, Emil Jellinek, who saw the possibility of developing a more profitable business. He visited Cannstatt, where he and Maybach discussed his ideas. The result was a car with a pressed steel frame, a radiator in front of the bonnet and magneto ignition, which looked quite unlike all other cars at that time. Jellinck was happy to invest in the company, but he felt there was prejudice against all things German in France, as there were still memories of the Franco–Prussian War. He suggested forming a new company under a different name and they called it after his daughter, Mercédès. The accents were dropped and one of the most famous names in motoring history was born.

Daimler died in 1900, but his name was destined to live on when he sold the patent rights to a British businessman, Frederick Simms, who formed the Daimler Company at a factory in Coventry. In 1926, the companies formed by the

The first Mercedes car built by Daimler.

two pioneers were united as Mercedes-Benz. It is ironic to most people that the name of the company is not remembered for either of the founding fathers, but the name of a rich banker's daughter.

The motor car was, for a century and more, generally regarded as a boon, but now we know that it has also been one of the leading factors in bringing about potentially devastating climate change. Ironically, we are now being asked to turn to electric cars as a new form of transport. However, an electric tricycle was built as early as 1882 and Londoners could hail an electric taxi cab in 1897, which had a range of 50 miles before it needed recharging.

But now, we shall leave the roads and head for the skies.

9

THE WRIGHT BROTHERS

The two brothers who designed and flew the world's first lighter-than-air powered aircraft.

Lighter-than-air craft had successfully developed from the first hot-air balloon through to the powered airship. They were, however, at a dead end. If progress was to be made in air transport, the future had to lie with heavier-than-air craft.

The idea of using wings to fly dates to prehistory, but the early versions nearly all depended on trying to emulate the birds, with flapping wings. The first successful attempts to make flying craft with fixed wings began in the nineteenth century, most importantly, with the work of Sir George Cayley.

Cayley was born in Scarborough in 1773, and it appears that his mother was the one who recognised his early interest in all things mechanical and ensured that the boy received an education in science and mathematics – unusual for a young aristocrat. In 1791, he went to live with a private tutor, a distinguished mathematician and Fellow of the Royal Society,

George Walker, with whom he studied mathematics – and became more than interested in his daughter, Sarah Walker, who was herself a highly competent mathematician. Lady Cayley decided her son needed a tutor with less-appealing offspring and so he was moved to study with another distinguished scientist, George Morgan, at Hackney College. In 1792, George's father died and he succeeded his father as a baronet and eventually, in 1795, he married Sarah.

Cayley's interest in aeronautics seems to have begun in 1792 and four years later, he made a model helicopter with four rotating propeller blades but recognised that it was impractical due to the lack of an appropriate engine. His first truly important work came in 1799, when he engraved his new idea on a silver disc – an idea that was vital to the future of aviation. He recognised that for an aeroplane to work it could not emulate the wings of a bird, which provided both lift and forward motion, but they would have to be separate – the wings providing lift and some other force moving the aircraft forward.

In 1804, he put this idea into practice when he built a model glider, a simple affair with a body made from a rod, wings formed by a kite and a tailpiece. Cayley published an account of flying it, 'If a velocity of 15 feet per second was given to it in an horizontal direction, it would skim for 20 to 30 yards supporting its own weight'.

Cayley continued to develop the idea of how a wing could provide lift, recognising for the first time the importance of the aerodynamic shape of a wing and indicating that he understood the general principle that lift was provided by the increased speed of air over the wing in comparison to the flow under it. This resulted in what he called a 'vacuity' above – in other words, the pressure above the wing was lower than that below, hence the lifting power. In 1808 he built a glider with a 300ft^2 wing and described the flight (*Nicholson's Journal*, 1810):

> It was very beautiful to see this noble white bird sail majestically from the top of a hill to any given point on the plain below it, according to the set of its rudder, merely by its own weight, descending at an angle of about 18 degrees with the horizon.

He would go on to make tests with gliders and towards the end of his life, in the 1850s, there are reports of manned flights, but no actual details have survived. Cayley was the first to try to understand the science behind manned flight, but it was some time before his ideas were put into practice to produce a fully controllable glider.

Otto Lilienthal flying with his early glider. (Library of Congress)

The most important developer was Otto Lilienthal, who was born in Germany in 1848 and was fascinated by the idea of flying from an early age, when he and his brother made wings for themselves, but failed to take off. In later life, he became a successful engineer and continued to develop his ideas about flight. He made his first flight in 1891 with what was, in effect, a form of hang-glider. He rested his body on a frame beneath the wing and controlled the flight by shifting his bodyweight. By 1894, he had developed his original model and set up his own test site by building a 15m-high artificial hill near his home, from which he could launch himself. This enabled him to make flights of over 300m. Altogether, he made around 2,000 flights and made similar gliders for individuals in many countries including the United States. His final flight was made on 9 August 1890, when the glider stalled and Lilienthal received injuries from which he died the following day.

* * *

The Wright brothers were born in Dayton, Ohio – Wilbur in 1867 and Orville in 1871. Their father was a bishop in the United Brethren Church, a radical protestant organisation that supported women's rights and opposed slavery and Freemasonry. He instilled in the boys a sense that they should learn to think for themselves, work hard and not take anything for granted. He even encouraged them to read books that contradicted his own deeply held religious views. They also had a younger sister, Katharine, who was to play an important part in their lives. Their two older brothers played only minor roles in the story – unlike the others, they married and left Dayton.

Wilbur was the livelier of the two brothers, an accomplished athlete and an excellent scholar, who had ambitions to

Orville and Wilbur Wright at the International Aviation Tournament, Belmont Park, Long Island, New York, in October 1910 (Cole & Co., Library of Congress)

study at Yale and might have done so but for an incident that occurred when he was 18. Another boy, Oliver Crook Haugh, apparently threw a hockey stick at Wilbur, which hit him in the face, and for weeks afterwards he suffered from pains in his jaw and had to be fitted with false teeth. It had a profound effect on Wilbur. He withdrew from the world and for three years did very little apart from read whatever he could find.

Meanwhile, Orville decided to take an interest in printing and worked for a time as an apprentice to a print firm while still at school. He set up his own homemade press at home and after a while the family were able to get him a small professional press to replace it. He decided to publish his own newspaper and his enthusiasm galvanised Wilbur to drag himself out of his long period of depression and join him in the work.

The first edition of the *West Side News* appeared in March 1889. Later, the title was changed to *The Item*. However, in 1891, they closed the paper and concentrated on working as jobbing printers.

Around this time, the two brothers became enthusiastic cyclists. They decided to open a cycle shop in 1893, but within two years were not just selling bicycles but manufacturing them – the old penny-farthings had been replaced by conventional machines with wheels of equal size, and their first bike with a tubular frame was named the Van Cleve. The business was prospering and things were going well, when, in 1896, Wilbur contracted typhoid and was close to death. He eventually recovered but in his convalescence, he read about the death of Lilienthal and began to study everything he could find about flight.

As a boy, he had already heard of the work of Cayley and had built several kites based on his design. Now he began to take the idea of manned flight seriously and he wrote to the

Smithsonian to tell them of his interest and to ask for copies of any paper that the institution had produced on aviation and a list of other works in English that might be helpful, ending the letter, 'I am an enthusiast not a crank in the sense that I have some pet theories as to the proper construction of a flying machine'.

The Smithsonian were helpful and among the works suggested were some by Octave Chanute, who had enjoyed a successful career as an engineer and a Professor of Physics at the Western University of Pennsylvania. In 1896, he had built a steam-powered, double-winged machine that was launched by catapult from a houseboat on the Potomac River and flew about half a mile before dropping into the river. He was to take an interest in the brothers' work over the next few years.

Wilbur recognised that for a flying machine, equilibrium was essential – Lilienthal had managed this by shifting his body to alter the angle of the glider. But Wilbur had a very different idea – he would emulate the birds by twisting the wings of a glider so that one wing would be at a different angle to the other, allowing the glider to make a banked turn. The system was known as 'wing warping'.

The next step was taken in 1899, when they began building an experimental kite. They had learned from Chanute that he considered a biplane to be the most stable form, so their kite was a biplane with a wing span of 50ft. The wing warping was controlled from the ground by sticks. The glider crashed, but the warping proved efficient, and so it was time to move on to a version that could be flown with a pilot on board.

The brothers now needed somewhere their flying machine could be tested, preferably with reliable winds and soft landings. They asked for advice from the Weather Bureau, which suggested that they should go to Kitty Hawk, on Bodie Island, off the coast of North Carolina, where there were

The Wright brothers with their experimental glider. (Library of Congress)

sandy beaches, sand hills for launching and steady winds of 10–20mph.

It seemed the ideal site, although it was some 700 miles away from their home and involved a lengthy voyage. The brothers constructed a new glider with an 18ft wingspan, which they hoped to fly themselves. It was to be sent in pieces to Kitty Wake and reassembled. There was a tent and camping equipment, tools and a camera.

Wilbur set off in 1900 for Elizabeth City, in North Carolina, where he hoped to get a boat to Kitty Wake, but it took four days before he met a man called Israel Perry, who was ready to take him. They set off on a skiff that seemed much the worse for wear, and when Wilbur mentioned it, he received the unwelcome news that the schooner they were going to was far worse. The voyage took two days, during which they weathered a storm, and they finally dropped anchor on

13 September. So began the journey towards powered flight that would make Kitty Wake famous.

Wilbur was soon at work setting up his machine and, as he wrote in a letter to his father, he had no intention of trying to put a motor in at that stage. He needed to find a machine that could be stable in flight first, and that would require trials. Orville arrived on 26 September, after a less-perilous crossing, and they got the glider ready for test flights.

The wings of the biplane were each 17ft by 5ft and the horizontal 'rudder' was at the front. It was mounted on skids not wheels. At first, they flew it using control lines from the ground and after the first successful attempt, it was caught in a gust of wind and had to be taken back to their camp to be reassembled.

In October, when they were due to go home, the glider was hauled across the dunes to the Kill Devil Hills sand dunes, the tallest of which was around 100ft high. From these, Wilbur made several manned flights, covering distances of up to 400ft. The glider was no longer needed, and so it was handed to the Tate family who had helped them, and Mrs Tate used the fabric to make dresses.

Back in Dayton, they once again took charge of their bicycle shop, but began to make plans for the next stage. The following year, they were visited by Octave Chanute, who offered them advice and brought a useful gift, an anemometer to give them accurate windspeed readings. As they prepared for their next visit to Kitty Wake, they hired Charles Taylor – usually known as Charlie – to run the shop in their absence with their sister.

In July 1901, they were off again, arriving at Elizabeth City just as a hurricane struck, so there was a delay before they could get to the island. They were now joined by two men from the Smithsonian who had been sent to help them.

The new glider was a larger version of the original, and the brothers had to build a shed to hold it, with a workshop attached and accommodation for all four men. Their timing was not good. The area had occasional plagues of mosquitos – and this turned out to be one of those occasions. Nothing could, it seemed, keep them away and Orville wrote that he was covered in bites 'the size of hens' eggs'.

On 27 July 1901, the first manned flights were begun with Wilbur at the controls. There were several adjustments to be made to stop the glider nose-diving and Wilbur had to keep moving further back until an equilibrium was achieved. Once that was settled, he made a successful flight of around 100 yards. But this was not as good as they had hoped and they found that although they had been following the information about wing shapes set out by the successful Lilienthal, the dimensions he had given proved not to work in practice. They realised that the only sure way to success was to make their own experiments on wing camber and rely on practical results, not academic papers. They decided that the curvature – the camber – of the wings was wrong and they changed it, making the wing far flatter. The result was a success. In Wilbur's own words, 'The operator could cause it almost to skim the ground.' They now had exactly what they wanted, a controllable machine. But there were problems – the wing warping was not answering expectations, and the brothers were convinced that somewhere there was a flaw in their system that needed to be eliminated. They headed back to Dayton to think about what to do next.

They decided they needed more experimental data. They built themselves a primitive wind tunnel out of a 6ft-long wooden box. They used hacksaw blades cut to different shapes and sizes to simulate wings and varied the 'windspeed' until they were happy they had the right shape, and then it was back to Kitty Hawk again for more trial flights.

There was one incident that could have been serious, when the less-experienced Orville took control and crashed. But fortunately, neither pilot nor glider was seriously damaged. There was to be one further adjustment, the rear rudder would be made moveable and could be controlled by the pilot at the same time as he altered the wing warping, by moving his hips to shift a hip cradle. When that succeeded, everything was now ready for the final phase to prepare for powered flight.

Finding an appropriate motor was the next problem to be solved. They tried the newly established car manufacturers, but any available engine was far too heavy, so they turned instead to their own ingenious mechanic, Charlie Taylor. He at once set about building a motor – something he had never attempted before. He solved the weight problem by using an aluminium cylinder block instead of iron. That just left one item to design – the propeller.

As described earlier, ships' propellers had been in use for about a century, but that did not mean that there was useful information on how one would work on an aeroplane. Once again, the brothers set about what they did best – their own painstaking experimental programme. Eventually, they found the right formula for pitch and shaped two propellers by hand. These were set between the wings, one of which was to turn clockwise and the other anticlockwise. The motor was fixed next to the pilot.

With everything organised, they prepared for the return to Kitty Hawk, where the plane would have to be built. In September 1903, they built an enlarged shed at Kitty Hawk and began the long process of assembling the machine – the first time it had all been put together – but not without several problems, which included having to send for new propeller shafts and braving some atrocious weather, from fierce gales to snow. A wooden track was laid for launching.

On 14 December 1903, everything was ready to go, and the brothers flipped a coin. Wilbur won and had the honour of being the first to pilot the plane.

It seemed to be working perfectly, but Wilbur made a mistake. The ascent was too steep, and it nose-dived back to earth. Repairs were made, and on 17 December, Orville took the controls. This time, although the flight was short, a mere 120ft from take-off, it had flown. More flights were made that day and on the fourth test, Wilbur flew for over half a mile and reached an altitude of over 800ft. It was a triumph.

The news was sent to Dayton by telegram and was taken to the editor of the *Dayton Daily Journal*, who was unimpressed and didn't bother to mention it in the next edition, thus losing the honour of being the first paper to report an epoch-making event.

When the brothers returned home, they decided that if they were going to continue developing what was now known as the flying machine, they would need to find somewhere more convenient than Kitty Hawk. They found what they were looking for in an 84-acre field at Huffman Prairie, 8 miles from Dayton.

They built *Flyer II* and began testing in May 1904. There were inevitably teething troubles, and one serious accident, when Orville was at the controls and a sudden gust of wind sent them crashing into the ground. The problem of taking off was solved by a form of catapult, using a tall tower. Weights were hauled to the top and attached to the launching trolley. Once the weights were dropped, the trolley shot along and *Flyer* took off. By September, Wilbur had flown half a mile and turned the plane through a half-circle.

The first powered flight at Kill Devil Hills in 1903. (NASA)

Orville Wright piloting the 1905 *Flyer* over Huffman Prairie.
(Library of Congress)

The brothers had hoped to persuade the US government to fund their planes, but it was the British who were the first to take an interest. Lieutenant Colonel Capper arrived in Dayton to discuss purchasing a plane. The British Army had already invested in aviation in the form of the Balloon Corps, founded in 1874. The brothers showed him photographs of their flights but were not yet ready for full-scale demonstrations. By this time, however, they had made significant progress in control and were able to turn the *Flyer*. To mark President Roosevelt's election, Wilbur flew three circles round the field.

A formal request to the US government was turned down and the British negotiations faltered, but there was now a positive response from France and a French delegation arrived in Dayton in 1906 to make arrangements. As a result, it was agreed that Wilbur should go to Paris to start negotiations, while Orville stayed behind to complete the construction of *Flyer III*. When that was complete, he and the machine would join Wilbur in France.

They had little success in the business negotiations, and now French engineers were beginning to work on aircraft of their own, notably the Voisin brothers. Wilbur returned to the United States and the brothers began making plans for their first public demonstrations using their new plane, *Flyer III*.

They had not flown for some time, so before returning to France, they went to Kitty Wake to perfect their technique. In May 1908, they arrived in France, only to discover that *Flyer III* had suffered considerable damage and there was an inevitable delay before they could show the French exactly what they could do. As a result, the first flight was postponed until August 1908.

The site chosen for the public flight was a racecourse at Le Mans, where, in front of a big crowd, Wilbur took off and completed two full circles above the course, before coming down to land. There were to be more successful demonstration flights, and Katharine, who had joined them in France, finally got to join her brothers as an aviator in February 1909, when she flew as a passenger. There was one unfortunate incident, when Wilbur made a mistake, the plane crashed and was damaged, but he was unharmed.

Shortly afterwards, they returned to the United States, and on reaching Dayton, they were given an ecstatic welcome. Crowds lined the streets as they were driven in a procession of carriages back to their home. They now had to prepare for their American demonstration.

The site was to be Fort Myer, Virginia, just across the Potomac River from Washington. Orville made a whole succession of record-breaking flights, culminating in flights lasting more than an hour, and on one occasion, he completed fifty-seven circles before coming down to land. On 17 September 1908, there was a request from Lieutenant Thomas Selfridge of the Signals Corps Aviation Board for a flight with Orville. It was agreed, and at first, everything seemed to be going well, but then a piece of a propeller broke off and the craft nosedived into the ground. Orville was injured and was left with one leg shorter than the other, but tragically the young lieutenant was killed.

Wilbur was to make several more flights over the years, including a flight round the famous Statue of Liberty. In May 1912, Wilbur contracted typhoid fever and died on the 30th. Orville continued flying but he gave up in 1918 at the age of 41 and sold the Wright Company the same year. He lived on until 1948 – long enough to see the aviation industry transformed beyond anything the brothers could have imagined.

There was one dark feature of the period. The brothers had offered the 1903 *Flyer* to the Smithsonian but incredibly, they had been turned down, and it was sent on loan to the London

Science Museum instead. There is a hint of intellectual snobbery in this, as the Smithsonian had supported Langley's unsuccessful machine and could not quite accept that two bicycle mechanics could have achieved what their own highly qualified scientist had singularly failed to achieve. In 1914, the Langley machine was taken out of storage and given another trial, which was moderately successful, at which point they claimed the honour of building the first successful powered aircraft. It soon transpired that many alterations had, in fact, been made to the Langley and when it was restored to its original condition, it failed dismally – honour was restored to the Wrights. Eventually, their *Flyer* was brought back from London and this time accepted by the Smithsonian.

The Wright brothers' success is the more remarkable in that they never had the backing of any organisation. What they did have, however, was a clear understanding that success came from methodical hard work. They had recognised that there was no point in a plane unless it proved to be possible to control the flight. So, they had set out on their long road of experimentation, moving from kite to glider to *Flyer I*. They faced many setbacks, but each time something went wrong, they patiently worked out why and set about finding the remedy, discovering along the way that allegedly 'scientific' information on flight might look convincing on paper but too often proved useless in practice. Their success was eventually acclaimed – and that acclamation was hard won and thoroughly deserved.

10

SIR FRANK WHITTLE

Frank Whittle was born in 1907 in Coventry, where his father worked as foreman in a factory manufacturing machine tools. The aircraft industry was scarcely in existence, yet Whittle remembers being given a toy aircraft, worked by clockwork, which never flew but the propeller whizzed round. Whether that was the start of his fascination for flying or not, he was to become obsessed with the idea of being a pilot from a very early age. He went to the local elementary school at the age of 5, and when he was 7 and war broke out, his interest in aircraft became more intense. One dramatic event occurred around that time, when an aircraft crash-landed near his home, and he rushed to see it and was able to watch it take off again.

In 1916, his father, Moses Whittle, was able to start up in business on his own by buying the Leamington Valve & Piston Ring Company and the family moved to Leamington Spa. Frank did well at primary school and won a scholarship to the local grammar school. But the family business was by now far from successful and they simply could not afford the fees, so he went instead to Leamington College, where the scholarship grant of £10 helped cover the expenses. This was not his only education; he was given simple tasks in his father's workshop and became familiar with the use of various types of machinery. He was also an enthusiastic reader, especially in the sciences – and he was able to use the local reference library to read widely on a variety of subjects, especially aviation, and it was during this time that he first came across a book on gas turbines.

Before continuing to look at Whittle's early life, this is a good time to look at the gas turbine itself. The first patent was taken out by an English inventor, John Barber, in 1791. It contained the main elements – a compressor, a combustor and a driving turbine. In this model, the gas was to be mixed with air, compressed in cylinders, then passed into the combustion chamber and ignited, after which the exhaust gas was to drive the vanes of a paddle wheel. It was not a very practical device, and it would be some time before a turbine would find a use in transport.

It was to be a century later when the next real advance was made by Charles Parsons. He was a junior partner in an engineering company manufacturing electric generators and he recognised that a turbine would be a more efficient method of turning a dynamo than the reciprocating steam engines then in use. He developed the idea that a turbine would also be an excellent way to provide smooth motion to move a propeller at high speed and would be ideal for developing faster warships.

In 1894, Parsons set up the Marine Steam Turbine Company and began developing an experimental vessel, *Turbinia*. The first version had a single turbine, in which high-pressure steam was passed through alternating rings of fixed and moving

Statue of Air Commodore Sir Frank Whittle in his uniform outside the
Coventry Transport Museum.

blades and powered a single propeller. The first results were disappointing and tests showed that the problem was the single propeller, which caused a cavitation effect in the water.

Parsons replaced the original with a triple-expansion turbine, driving three propellers. Steam at 200psi was passed first to the high-pressure turbine on the starboard side, then to the intermediate-pressure turbine, and the exhaust from that went to the final, low-pressure turbine, producing 2,000 shaft horsepower. In a demonstration run at the Spithead Review of 1897, the sleek craft sped across the fleet at an unprecedented 34 knots. She was to be the forerunner of the torpedo boat.

Parsons then developed a turbine with reduction gearing that could be used for bigger ships and, in 1906, the first turbine battleship was launched. But it was the ability of a turbine to produce speeds in excess of those derived from the older reciprocating engines that would later inspire Whittle.

At the age of 15, Frank Whittle applied to join the RAF but was rejected on the grounds of physical fitness – he was just 5ft tall at the time and not very muscular. Several months later, he had grown 3in taller and had been exercising hard. But once again, he was turned down. He was to make one final attempt, but this time, instead of returning to Halton, where he had been twice rejected, he went to RAF Cranwell to apply for training as an apprentice. It was third time lucky: at the age of 16, he had started on the journey towards achieving his ambition of becoming a pilot.

Whittle spent three years training as an apprentice. He hated the discipline, which often appeared mindlessly brutal, but did well in the academic work. He was an enthusiastic member of the model aircraft society and headed a team on what was their most ambitious project – a model plane with a 10ft wingspan powered by a small petrol engine. This brought him to the attention of Wing Commander Barton, who was instrumental in getting him accepted at the end of his apprenticeship to join the RAF College as a cadet. This was the vital turning point – he was now officially passed for aircrew training.

He was now entering a very different world, finding himself with his working-class background in a society dominated by former public schoolboys. He was required not only to learn to fly but to act as 'an officer and a gentleman'. Bizarrely, things had not changed that much when I was called up for National Service and was assessed both for suitability for aircrew and officer material – and after selection, I found that as a cadet, I too was surrounded by ex-public schoolboys. I had the advantage of having already been to university, but I can imagine how strange it must have been for Whittle to adapt to his new life. But at last,

The Avro 504K in which Whittle did his early flying. (Airwolfhead, CC SA 2.0 via Wikimedia Commons)

he was to receive flying lessons in an Avro 504K biplane and after just five and a half hours of dual control, he went solo in his second term.

Whittle's early flying career was certainly not without incident. On one occasion, he got lost and decided to land in what appeared to be a suitable green field, only to discover that his plane was embedded in mud. With the help of a farmhand, he was able to take off again but only succeeded in hitting a tree. Not only had he written off the plane, but he had broken a rule that as a cadet he should not attempt to take off after a forced landing. Later, he was caught low-flying over Seaford, again breaking regulations.

He may have written off a plane, but his studies were going particularly well and one of the tasks set to the cadets was to write a thesis each term. In his fourth term, he wrote a paper on future developments in aircraft design. His argument was that high speeds could only be achieved at higher altitudes than were currently possible with existing craft, as air resistance was reduced. He also suggested that the speeds he was proposing were impossible with existing engines and could only be achieved by using some form of gas turbine – although at this stage, he was still thinking of it as driving a propeller. It was an idea that he would continue to consider over the next few years.

In the meantime, he was showing exceptional skill as a pilot and was an expert at what was then known as 'crazy flying' – what we would now call aerobatics. He had hoped to be awarded the prize as best pilot of the year but was denied it on the grounds of 'dangerous flying', even though he had given a superb display which had been officially approved. Nevertheless, he did get the award for Aeronautical Science and left Cranwell in 1928 as Pilot Officer Whittle and a qualified pilot.

He joined a fighter squadron at Hornchurch in Essex and, once again, he was spotted flying low and doing aerobatics off Canvey Island. As this was the second offence, he could have been in very serious trouble. A complaint had been made to the police by a family on the island who had seen Whittle and another pilot's antics. The two pilots called on the family, abjectly apologised and the police case was dropped.

His next move was to Flying Instruction School at Wittering, where he could qualify as an instructor. High-speed flying was very much in the news as the Supermarine seaplane with an improved Rolls-Royce engine had just won the Schneider Trophy at a new record average speed of 328.6mph – but the design was not appropriate for military aircraft, largely because the plane could only run for a very short time and used a special fuel mix. It did, however, bring Whittle back to thinking about the gas turbine.

He discussed his ideas with Flying Officer W.E.P. Johnson, who had been a patent officer before taking a short-service commission. Johnson was enthusiastic and persuaded Whittle to bring his ideas to the Air Ministry, who dismissed the proposal as impractical. However, with Johnson's help, he filed an application for a patent for what would be the world's first turbojet. The patent details were presented in 1930 and the patent granted in 1932.

Whittle's next post was as a flying instructor at Digby in Lincolnshire, a task which gave him time to continue thinking about his turbojet. His stay there was enlivened when he was chosen, with another officer, to do a two-man demonstration of 'crazy flying' at the famous Hendon Airshow. With Johnson's help, he also got an interview with a commercial company, British Thomson-Houston (BTH) to discuss his ideas for a turbojet. The company were encouraging but felt that they would need a minimum of £60,000 for development, which was more than they were prepared to risk.

After just a year at Digby, he received a far more exciting posting as a test pilot on float boats at Felixstowe. He was soon involved in being catapulted off HMS *Pegasus*, but unlike a later generation of aircraft carriers, there were no facilities for landing back on deck. He had to land on water and make his way back to the ship to be pulled back on board – a process that he did not enjoy, as he bounced through the waves.

There was one hair-raising episode in 1932, when he was flying a Fairey IIIF off the *Ark Royal*, with a Flight Lieutenant Kirk as a passenger behind him. As he took off, the nose dipped, and looking round, he found his passenger lying on the tailplane, holding on to the fin. Somehow, he had lost his grip on the edge of the cockpit and been thrown backwards during the take-off. Whittle managed to land safely in the sea, narrowly avoiding flying into a passing ocean liner.

One of his more exacting tasks as a test pilot was to ditch the aircraft, which involved a pancake landing in the sea, dropping down from just a few feet above the waves, after which he scrambled out into a dinghy. It was even more dangerous for Whittle, who had never learned to swim.

During his time testing float planes, he was still developing his ideas on jet propulsion, but when that period came to an end, he was back to studying, this time at the Officers' School of Engineering at RAF Henlow. He did exceptionally well and was selected to take a two-year engineering course at Cambridge University. This would normally have been a three-year course, but because of his previous experience, he skipped the first year. He was to graduate with a first-class degree.

During his time at Cambridge, the question of renewing his patent came up, which he was reluctant to do, having had so little success in interesting the Air Ministry in his ideas. He might well have dropped the idea altogether had he not received a letter from Rolf Dudley Williams, who he had known at Cranwell, saying that he knew of an engineering firm who might be interested in his idea for developing the jet engine. A meeting was arranged with Williams and another former RAF pilot, J.C.B. Tinling, who were partners in a firm manufacturing cigarette machines. It was agreed that they would cover the costs of securing patents in exchange for a quarter share each in a successful enterprise. To move on to building a prototype would, they estimated, cost £50,000 – money that, at the time, none of them had. Finance would need to be raised.

Three new patents were drafted, but they needed the approval of the Air Ministry, which insisted on being a free Crown user and therefore, in practice, the main, if not only customer – not something that would encourage private backers. However, a new interested party now appeared on the scene, M.L. Bramson, considered an expert in aeronautical engineering. Through him, a meeting was arranged with investment bankers O.T. Falk. Agreement was reached to form a company, but they still needed RAF approval to allow Whittle to be involved. This was settled when the President of the Air Council entered the partnership, and a company was duly formed in 1936 called Power Jets Ltd. There was, however, one stipulation: Whittle would be chief engineer but was not to spend more than six hours a week on the project, as he was still a serving officer. Meanwhile, Whittle had made contact again with British Thomson-Houston for the manufacture of a trial bench engine with the understanding that if successful, they would also be responsible for manufacturing later engines. The idea that Whittle had kept in his mind for so long was about to become a reality, although not without overcoming many problems.

The first engine tests were begun at BTH in 1937 with the 'WE' (Whittle engine). The results were often alarming, with the engine running out of control and sheets of flame appearing as the combustion chamber became red hot. Most of those working with the engine took off as fast as they could go, leaving Whittle to bring things back under control. At the time, there were disagreements between Whittle and the BTH engineers and money was rapidly running out. After a good deal of financial wrangling, funds were obtained, and work could continue.

Whittle had completed his course at Cambridge, had been allowed by the RAF to work full time on the project and was promoted to squadron leader. The next set of tests on the completely rebuilt engine were to take place in a former BTH foundry at Lutterworth, near Rugby.

Things did not always go well in the relationship between the BTH engineers and Whittle, particularly over the design of the turbine blades. Eventually, however, the rebuilt engine was ready for testing at Lutterworth and ran for one hour and forty-five minutes before there was a catastrophic failure of the turbine. During that time, however, the engine ran at 13,000rpm and it was possible to measure the thrust for the first time at 480lb.

Later modifications included abandoning the single combustion chamber in favour of ten smaller ones, and by using interconnecting tubes, it was only necessary to ignite one tube, which would then ignite the others. After a long series of tests and adjustments, the engine finally ran at 14,500rpm in 1939.

As always, the plans for moving forward were hampered by lack of finance. There was still the hope that the Air Ministry

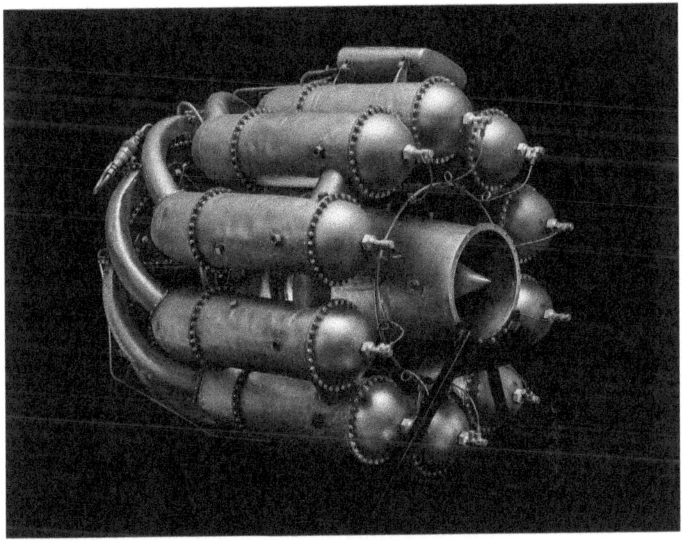

The Whittle 1X engine, now preserved in the National Air & Space Museum, Washington DC, United States.

would order a plane from Power Jets, which would then contract out the manufacture to an appropriate company, and Whittle had already had talks with Gloster about this. The company had been formed in 1917 and had produced the very successful Bristol Fighter. Although it retained the name, the company was actually taken over by Hawker Aircraft in 1934, when they produced the famous Gloster Gladiator. But everything still depended on the Air Ministry being interested.

In January 1940, Air Vice Marshal Tedder, Director General of Research and Development, and Sir Henry Tizard, Chairman of the Aeronautical Research Committee, visited Power Jets to see a demonstration of the engine. It was clear, however, that more development work was needed, and work was already in hand for the development of 'W2', which would have an increased power output of 1600lb. But there was now increasing tension between Whittle and the engineers of BTH, who had their own ideas of how a turbine should be designed, which differed considerably from Whittle's.

In looking around for a new contractor, Whittle was introduced to Maurice Wilks, Chief Engineer of Rover Cars. There now began a complex series of negotiations, between Power Jets, the Air Ministry and Rover, in which Whittle felt that his company was likely to be the loser. In the event, the co-operation between the various parties floundered on for a long time, while work proceeded on two engines – the W2 being manufactured by BTH and another, the W2B, produced by Rover. Finally, plans were completed to fit an engine into a new plane, the E28, for test flights.

In April 1941, Gloster's chief test pilot, P.E.G. Sayer, began the trials, beginning with taxiing, and once these had proved successful, the first flight was planned to take place at RAF Cranwell. It was from there that Sayer took off in the E28 for a flight that lasted for seventeen minutes. This historic moment was never captured on film, simply because the Air Ministry, despite requests from everyone, declined to send anyone down to record the historic event.

During subsequent flights, the plane reached speeds of 370mph in level flight, surpassing what was then the fastest plane in the RAF, the Spitfire. Plans for further development were not helped by the fact that although Whittle and Power Jets had been responsible for all the design work on the engine and were expected to provide all necessary information to the contractors for building, there were no restraints on the latter. Whittle's health suffered from the stress and anxiety.

In 1941, the United States heard about the new developments and the W1X engine was flown over to the United States, together with a team of experts from Power Jets.

The E28/39 in flight. (Dane A. Penland/Air Historical Branch-RAF/MOD [OGL v.1.0])

Agreement was quickly reached, and unlike the British officials, the Americans wasted no time in going ahead with constructing engines and made plans to install them in a new aircraft built by Bell Aircraft – and within a year the Bell jets were flying.

In Britain, relations between Bristol and Whittle deteriorated when it transpired that Bristol had been making substantial design changes, and contrary to all agreements, had done so without consulting either Power Jets or Air Ministry officials. In 1942, Whittle left for the United States, where he was able to offer considerable help in developing their jet plane, but on his return to England, he faced yet more problems.

He was summoned to the Ministry of Air Power, where he was in effect told that they considered the W2B engine being developed at Bristol was an abject failure and it was his fault. He strenuously rejected the accusation, pointing out that Bristol had made the changes without consultation and against his express wishes. It marked the end of the Bristol involvement in the project. A deal was struck, and it was decided that Rover would be replaced by Rolls-Royce.

There was to be one further twist in the tale of Power Jets and the government. In 1943, plans were announced to take the company into public ownership. After long discussion, it was agreed that compensation would be paid of slightly more than £130,000. None of this was to go to Whittle personally, who had surrendered his shares to the Ministry of Power. He was, however, promoted to the rank of air commodore.

Whittle's greatest satisfaction was the delivery of the first British jet fighter, the Gloster Meteor, to the RAF in 1944. It was only after the end of the war in Europe that Whittle was able to climb into the cockpit and actually fly a Meteor – an experience that, unsurprisingly, he found exhilarating. He was later to receive a grant of £10,000 in recognition of his unique contribution to aeronautics, but his working involvement was coming to an end. In 1946, he retired from Power Jets and two years later, from the RAF. Honours came to him later in life, including a knighthood and the Order of Merit, and in the United States he was recognised with a place in the International Hall of Fame. He died in 1996 at the age of 89.

This account can only give a hint at the machinations between the various parties that plagued Whittle throughout his time working on the engine. Had he received the support he needed from the start, there can be little doubt that development would have been a good deal faster. He was having to grapple with brand-new technical problems of design and finding the right materials, while all the time constantly having to deal with lack of money and fractious arguments.

That he succeeded is a miracle of perseverance. He lived to see the airlines of the world using planes powered by jet engines – and even to see arguably the most beautiful aircraft ever built – Concorde – carry passengers across the Atlantic at supersonic speed. Yet when he first had his idea of high-altitude fast aircraft, he was flying in biplanes with fuselages covered in fabric. There has probably never been a more dramatic and speedy revolution in transport than that.

Gloster Meteor T7. (R. McDonald, CCA 2.0)

EPILOGUE

The ten pioneers chosen for this book could scarcely be more disparate, yet all had one thing in common – an ability to think independently and, if necessary, to ignore 'expert' advice. Of all the developments that came from their inventive minds, the one that has had the longest impact is the marine chronometer. Until the arrival of satellites and global positioning systems (GPS), navigation still depended on an accurate chronometer and a sextant.

The steam age has gone and although we can still enjoy a trip in a paddle steamer or ride on a preserved steam railway, they are exercises in delightful nostalgia and have little to do with the everyday business of getting from A to B. Similarly, we can enjoy a flight in a hot-air balloon, but the age of the airship has ended. The world is full of cars powered by internal combustion engines, but it does seem that their days are numbered – and must be, to avoid catastrophic global warming. Electric power for transport, on the other hand, is now being seen as the answer to that same problem.

We can see where our existing transport systems seem to be going and what are the likeliest lines of development. What we do not know is what ideas might, even now, be forming in some inventive mind. In the realms of science fiction, space travel is commonplace. Will that be the next transport revolution? Not just sending individuals to land on the Moon or perhaps a planet, but regular movement between Earth and new extraterrestrial settlements in the way that we can fly easily between continents?

Or will the change be something so startlingly new that we cannot at this stage even imagine what it might be? One thing is certain – this is not the end of the story. There is a new chapter waiting to be written; we just don't know what or when it will be.

FURTHER READING

Adler, Dennis, *Daimler and Benz: The Complete History* (HarperCollins, 2005).

Baker, Matthew, *Fragments of Ancient Shipwrighting* (1586).

Burton, Anthony, *Balloons and Airships: A Tale of Lighter Than Air Aviation* (Pen & Sword, 2019).

Burton, Anthony, *Richard Trevithick* (Aurum Press, 2000).

Cole, S.M., 'Early Forms of Society' in Singer, Charles, E.J. Holmyard & A.R. Hall (eds), *A History of Technology*, Volume 1 (Oxford University Press, 1954).

Corlett, Ewan, *The Iron Ship: The Story of Brunel's SS Great Britain* (Moonraker Press, 1975).

Dumpleton, Bernard, *The Story of the Paddle Steamer* (ePub, Melksham, 2002).

Golley, John, Frank Whittle & Bill Gunston (ed.), *Genesis of the Jet: Frank Whittle and the Invention of the Jet Engine* (Airlife Publishing, 1996).

McCullough, David, *The Wright Brothers* (Simon & Schuster, 2015).

Rees, Abraham, *The Cyclopaedia: Universal Dictionary of Arts, Sciences and Literature* (Longman, 1819).

Rolt, L.T.C., *Between Two Seas* (Euromapping, 1994).

Siemens Historical Institute, *Shaping the Future: The Siemens Entrepreneurs 1847–2018* (Siemens Historical Institute, 2018).

Singer, Charles, E.J. Holmyard, A.R. Hall & T.I. Williams (eds), *A History of Technology*, Volumes 3–7 (Oxford University Press, 1957–78).

Sobel, Dava, *Longitude: The True Story of a Lone Genius Who Solved the Greatest Scientific Problem of His Time* (Fourth Estate, 1995).

Trevithick, Francis, *Life of Richard Trevithick* (E. & F.N. Spon, 1872).

Whittle, Sir Frank, *Jet: The Story of a Pioneer* (Frederick Mueller, 1953).

ACKNOWLEDGEMENTS

The author would like to thank the following for supplying photographs for this book:

Airwolfhead; Bin im Garten; Tom Brogden; Neil Crawford; Fronteras; The Masters and Fellows, Magdalene College, Cambridge; Martonvl; Robert Mason; R. McDonald; Stephen McKay; Dane A. Penland; The Steam Museum, Straffan, Ireland; Tournasol7; Trevithick Society; Peter Trimming; Colonel Warden; Wladyslav; The Wub.

INDEX